G000061527

# Hodder Cambridge Primary

# English

## Teacher's Pack
## Stage 1

**Eileen Jones**
Series Editor: Dr Wendy Jolliffe

**HODDER** EDUCATION
AN HACHETTE UK COMPANY

The Publishers would like to thank the following for permission to reproduce copyright material:

**Acknowledgements**
Pages 5–9 written by Moira Brown.

Every effort has been made to trace all copyright holders, but if any have been inadvertently overlooked the Publishers will be pleased to make the necessary arrangements at the first opportunity.

Although every effort has been made to ensure that website addresses are correct at time of going to press, Hodder Education cannot be held responsible for the content of any website mentioned in this book. It is sometimes possible to find a relocated web page by typing in the address of the home page for a website in the URL window of your browser.

Hachette UK's policy is to use papers that are natural, renewable and recyclable products and made from wood grown in sustainable forests. The logging and manufacturing processes are expected to conform to the environmental regulations of the country of origin.

Orders: please contact Bookpoint Ltd, 130 Milton Park, Abingdon, Oxon OX14 4SB. Telephone: +44 (0)1235 827720. Fax: +44 (0)1235 400454. Lines are open 9.00a.m.–5.00p.m., Monday to Saturday, with a 24-hour message answering service. Visit our website at www.hoddereducation.com

© Eileen Jones 2015
First published in 2015 by
Hodder Education,
An Hachette UK Company
Carmelite House
50 Victoria Embankment
London EC4Y 0DZ

Impression number    10 9 8 7 6
Year                 2019

All rights reserved. Apart from any use permitted under UK copyright law, no part of this publication may be reproduced or transmitted in any form or by any means, electronic or mechanical, including photocopying and recording, or held within any information storage and retrieval system, without permission in writing from the publisher or under licence from the Copyright Licensing Agency Limited. Further details of such licences (for reprographic reproduction) may be obtained from the Copyright Licensing Agency Limited, Saffron House, 6–10 Kirby Street, London EC1N 8TS.

Cover illustration by Sandy Lightley
Illustration by Marleen Visser
Typeset in Stone Informal in 11pt by Resolution
Printed in the UK by the CPI Group (UK) Ltd, Croydon, CR0 4YY

A catalogue record for this title is available from the British Library

ISBN 9781471831010

# Contents

## Introduction

## Term 1

## Term 2

## Term 3

# Introduction

## About the series

Hodder Cambridge Primary English is a series consisting of a Learner's book, Teacher's Pack and Workbook for each Cambridge Primary English curriculum stage.

The books are written by experienced primary practitioners to reflect the different teaching approaches recommended in the Cambridge Primary Teacher Guides and covering the Cambridge Primary English frameworks. The content of each book is outlined below.

### Learner's book

The structure and content of the Learner's books are based on the Cambridge Primary English framework for each stage. Each unit covers a reading genre from the English framework. There are nine units per Learner's book. Units contain:

- learning objectives
- *Helpful hints* boxes, which explain the focus of learning with examples
- *Did you know?* fact boxes
- model texts
- a glossary
- activities linked to reading, writing, and speaking and listening
- *Try this* challenge activities
- checklists for learning.

### Teacher's Pack

The Teacher's Packs support the activities in the Learner's books and Workbooks, and reinforce the learning through:

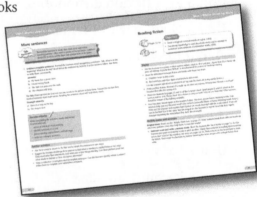

- unit objective overviews
- Learner's book activity notes and answers
- Workbook answers
- starter activities
- suggestions for success criteria
- further activities
- assessment ideas
- IT links
- book list for additional model texts.

### Workbook

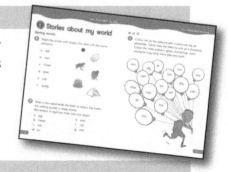

The Workbooks can be used for homework or extension activities after the relevant pages in the Learner's book are complete. The Workbooks either build on what has taken place during the lesson or challenge learners to develop their learning further through:

- exciting activities linked to the objectives in the Learner's book
- a self-assessment page at the end of each unit.

### How to use this series

This book, along with the Learner's book and Workbook, covers the Cambridge Primary curriculum framework for English at Stage 1. It should be worked through systematically to ensure complete coverage of the objectives for this stage. The activities are designed to build on previous knowledge as your class progresses through the Learner's book and Workbook.

# Assessment

## Learning objectives

An overview of all the objectives covered within a unit is given at the start of each chapter of teaching notes. The objectives (and codes) relevant to the Learner's book pages are also given at the start of each section of notes. At the start of each lesson, it is good practice to present the learning objective to the learners in child-friendly language. Learners should be clear on the focus of the lesson and what they are expected to learn. Some key objectives also appear in the Learner's book. At the end of the lesson you should refer back to these objectives to check the learners' understanding.

### Success criteria

In each section of teaching notes, suggestions for success criteria are given. The success criteria are used to assess the outcome of the learning that has taken place in each lesson. The success criteria are, in effect, what the successful learning will 'look' like, once the learning objectives have been met.

For example, if the learning objective was *Begin to vary sentence openings, e.g. with simple adverbs (2Wp5)*, the success criteria could be that learners selected the correct adverb to insert at the beginning of sentences. More would need to be covered on this objective for the learning to be fully embedded and understood.

For example, in subsequent lessons learners could: highlight simple adverbs in a text; choose adverbs from a word bank to use in their own sentences; recognise and use a wider range of adverbs, such as 'soon' and 'later'.

The success criteria should always be made clear to learners. Older learners could be encouraged to write down the success criteria at the top of their work. Marking should be related to the success criteria only. You could use a suggestion from the success criteria section in the teacher's notes to create task cards to make it clear to learners exactly what they have to do, and what success looks like. For example:

---

**Success criteria** ✓

Write six sentences using a capital letter and full stop correctly.

**What you have to do**
- Sort the words and full stops written on the card into six sentences.
- Copy the sentences into your book.

**Tip**
Remember to have a capital letter at the beginning of each sentence and a full stop at the end. All your sentences should make sense!

---

### Activity notes and answers

Within the teaching notes, a bold statement at the start of each activity shows the focus of the learning and this is linked to the objectives and success criteria. In some instances, it may be difficult to check if the success criteria have been achieved, for example, if there are large groups of children working together or they are not reporting directly to you. In these cases, watch the learners carefully and note any who have difficulties. If you observe any pairs working well, ask them to model the learning for others.

## Formative assessment

Formative assessment is a form of on-going assessment that occurs in every lesson and informs the teacher and learners of the progress they are making, linked to the success criteria. The success criteria section in the teacher's notes supports teachers in making formative assessments as the learners complete the activities in the Learner's book and Workbook.

One of the advantages of formative assessment is that any issues of learning that emerge during the lesson can be responded to immediately. For example, if learners are asked to display their written answers, the teacher can see at a glance whether the learning objective has been understood. If necessary, more time can be given to consolidating the objective before moving on. Ways of finding out about learning during the lesson need to be quick and unobtrusive. For example, you could build a two-minute slot into the lesson where learners are able to ask questions and pursue misconceptions, or learners are asked to give a signal to show their understanding.

Formative assessment will also influence the next step in learning, and may influence changes in planning and/or delivery for subsequent lessons. An end-of-lesson plenary can be used to find out more about learning. For example, learners could list what they have or have not understood on sticky notes, or simply be asked some questions by the teacher to clarify their understanding of the objectives. The start of the next lesson might be used to revisit an objective and, on occasion, extend to the whole lesson. Assessment decisions such as these ensure that teaching is in line with learning, and not the other way around.

## Summative assessment

Summative assessment is essential at the end of each unit of work to assess at a key point in time exactly what the learners know, understand and can do. The end-of-unit quizzes in the Learner's books and self-assessment pages in the Workbooks form part of the summative assessment process. Further assessment ideas within the teaching notes are designed to provide teachers with a variety of opportunities to check the learners' understanding of the unit. These activities can include specific questions for teachers to ask, activities for the learners to carry out (independently, in pairs or in groups) or written assessment.

The information gained from both the formative and summative assessment ideas should be used to inform future planning in order to close any gaps in the learners' understanding as recommended by *Assessment for Learning* (AFL). Assessment is no longer viewed as something separate, but built-in to the fabric of planning, teaching and learning.

# Strategies for differentiation

## What is differentiation?

Differentiation is the adjustment of the teaching and learning process so that the different needs of the learners can be accommodated, and individual learning maximised. The differentiation ideas on the following pages are designed to support the activities in the Learner's book and Workbook. The ideas are split into reading and writing strategies, with suggestions for the more-able and support for the less-able learners.

### High Frequency Words and Common Irregular Words

The High Frequency Words and Common Irregular Words referred to in this Teacher's Pack, the Learner's book and Workbook are words that learners need to be able to read and spell by the end of the stage. Refer to pages 10–11 for a list of the High Frequency and Common Irregular Words for Stage 1. Some of these words cannot be easily segmented into **phonemes** or **letter strings**, and therefore just have to be learnt.

### Expert Learner

The Expert Learner referred to in the differentiation ideas on the following pages is a learner who is considered to be secure in the activity task or learning objective.

### Reading for understanding

The differentiation ideas in the Reading for understanding column on the following pages focus on learners' comprehension and understanding of texts, and how to read effectively for meaning.

### Text features

The differentiation ideas in the Text features column on the following pages focus on how texts are organised, structured and developed.

# Differentiation ideas for less-able learners

## READING

| Reading skills | Reading for understanding | Text features |
|---|---|---|
| • Teacher segments some sentences from the text into phonemes, e.g. A cat on a big bed /a/ /c/a/t/ /o/n/ /a/ /b/i/g/ /b/e/d/.<br>Ask the learners to say the words emphasising the segments before blending them to read the sentences.<br>• Teacher writes high frequency words from the text on the board for reference, segmenting as appropriate. Learners could sort the words into phonemes and/or spelling patterns.<br>• Learner discusses words in the text not understood with an 'expert learner' and then clarifies words still not understood with the teacher. | • Teacher models reading to the punctuation mark, emphasising key words. Learners to copy this technique.<br>• Learner uses a 'What if I don't know a word' prompt card. These cards provide tips for reading such as:<br>  o split the word into phonemes, patterns or syllables<br>  o try reading the whole sentence and then reread it<br>  o look at the punctuation marks for a clue<br>  o look for clues in the illustration<br>  o think of something you have read already that will give you a clue.<br>• Teacher models scanning (to find specific information): learner to be shown how to move the eye quickly across and down the page, using a pen or finger to help 'steer' it.<br>• Teacher models skimming (to find main ideas): learner shown how a pencil or finger can be used to help 'push' the eye across 7–9 words at a time, only pausing on punctuation marks. | • Learner answers easier questions, focused on location and retrieval of literal information, e.g. when, what, who.<br>• Learner provides visual answers, e.g. drawings, mind maps, flow diagrams, plot graphs, cartoons, storyboards, annotated drawings of a character.<br>• Learner works with an 'expert learner', giving statements about a character and scanning a short piece of text for the supporting quote.<br>• Learner acts out a one-minute summary of the story and then writes it down.<br>• Learner given key words/phrases to discuss with an 'expert learner' and locates them in the text. The learners then read the text in turns.<br>• Learner uses partially completed answer frames to respond to a more difficult text. |

## WRITING

| Spelling skills | Grammar and punctuation | Text features |
|---|---|---|
| • Learner keeps a spelling journal, e.g. a list of high frequency words, individual spelling targets, phoneme lists.<br>• Learner uses synonym banks for well-used words such as *said, went, got* and *nice* or other words in the text.<br>• Teacher alerts learner to key words in a text prior to completing the task.<br>• Teacher provides vocabulary/word banks on particular writing tasks. Learner to tick/highlight each time they use these words in their writing. | • Learner retells the story in one minute without using *and, then*. (This will only work if learners speak in sentences!)<br>• Learner given a target number regarding the use of *and, then* in a writing piece.<br>• Learner provided with a bank of straightforward subordinating connectives to use in their writing, e.g. *because, although, if, since, when.*<br>• Learner allowed to make capital letters very large at the beginning of sentences and to highlight all punctuation marks. | • Teacher provides a 'Question plan' grid for story planning: *Who is in the story? Where does it take place? When does it happen? What happens? How does it end?*<br>• Learner uses five paragraph boxes and writes a sentence in each box to show what is going to happen in a story. This plan is then used to inform the writing of the story.<br>• Teacher provides the first sentence of each paragraph of the story in a writing frame for the learner to complete.<br>• Learners given a different outcome to the activity, e.g. instead of writing a story, be required to write the opening and then a bullet point plan to show what the rest of the story will be about. |

# Differentiation ideas for more-able learners

| READING | | |
| --- | --- | --- |
| **Reading skills** | **Reading for understanding** | **Text features** |
| • Learner finds spelling patterns in a text for specified phonemes, e.g. 'ow' – how, now.<br><br>• Learner collects words with a particular phoneme and sorts these according to the different spellings, e.g. /ee/ – written as 'tree', 'me', meat, happy, etc.<br><br>• Learner works in a pair with less-able child to demonstrate how to blend phonemes in words, e.g. 'ship' – /sh/i/p/.<br><br>• Learner selects different words for 'said' or another selected common word using a word bank. | • Learner explains how a character feels in a story by speaking as if the character, or moving as if the character.<br><br>• Learner creates a 'guess who I am' activity by talking about a well-known character in a story for other children to guess.<br><br>• Learner is given a range of why, who, what and how questions related to a story and has to explain to a partner, or the class.<br><br>• Learner reads a section of text to the class with expression, having practised with a partner.<br><br>• Learner has to summarise to a partner what a page of text read is about. | • Learner writes a few words in thought bubbles to explore a character's feelings.<br><br>• Learner collects words, for example, that rhyme or have alliteration for a class display.<br><br>• Learner collects more information about a character and creates a poster with a picture of the character with labels to denote characteristics, e.g. happy/sad face, etc.<br><br>• Learner writes words in speech bubbles for characters to show how they speak, e.g. grumpy: 'Go away!'<br><br>• Learner finds other texts by the same author and reads with an adult. |

| WRITING | | |
| --- | --- | --- |
| **Spelling skills** | **Grammar and punctuation** | **Text features** |
| • Learner selects alternative words from a word bank, e.g. other words for 'nice'.<br><br>• Learner creates a spelling journal. This could include: a list of high frequency words recently taught; individual words as spelling targets; ways of remembering tricky words (e.g. 'Sally Ann is dizzy' for 'said').<br><br>• Learners arrange words in alphabetical order by first letter.<br><br>• Learner works with a less-able child to help him/her find words related to a theme. | • Learner works with a less-able child to insert correct punctuation in a piece of text.<br><br>• In pairs, learners write dialogue as speech bubbles in a cartoon strip.<br><br>• Learner collects examples of connectives from texts.<br><br>• Learner improves simple sentences by adding adjectives, e.g. 'the dog barked' – 'the huge dog barked'.<br><br>• Learner practises reading sentences with correct expression according to punctuation. | • Learner writes further sentences of a narrative.<br><br>• Working in pairs, learners agree on an ending to a story, write it and then compare it.<br><br>• Learner annotates a non-fiction text to note the title, contents, page, sub-heading and shares with another learner. |

# First 100 High Frequency Words

In frequency order reading down the columns.

| the | that | not | look | put |
|-----|------|-----|------|-----|
| and | with | then | don't | could |
| a | all | were | come | house |
| to | we | go | will | old |
| said | can | little | into | too |
| in | are | as | back | by |
| he | up | no | from | day |
| I | had | mum | children | made |
| of | my | one | him | time |
| it | her | them | Mr | I'm |
| was | what | do | get | if |
| you | there | me | just | help |
| they | out | down | now | Mrs |
| on | this | dad | came | called |
| she | have | big | oh | here |
| is | went | when | about | off |
| for | be | it's | got | asked |
| at | like | see | their | saw |
| his | some | looked | people | make |
| but | so | very | your | an |

# Next 200 High Frequency Words

In frequency order reading down the columns.

| water | bear | find | these | live |
|---|---|---|---|---|
| away | can't | more | began | say |
| good | again | I'll | boy | soon |
| want | cat | round | animals | night |
| over | long | tree | never | narrator |
| how | things | magic | next | small |
| did | new | shouted | first | car |
| man | after | us | work | couldn't |
| going | wanted | other | lots | three |
| where | eat | food | need | head |
| would | everyone | fox | that's | king |
| or | our | through | baby | town |
| took | two | way | fish | I've |
| school | has | been | gave | around |
| think | yes | stop | mouse | every |
| home | play | must | something | garden |
| who | take | red | bed | fast |
| didn't | thought | door | may | only |
| ran | dog | right | still | many |
| know | well | sea | found | laughed |
| let's | fun | any | better | lived |
| much | place | under | hot | birds |
| suddenly | mother | hat | sun | duck |
| told | sat | snow | across | horse |
| another | boat | air | gone | rabbit |
| great | window | trees | hard | white |
| why | sleep | bad | floppy | coming |
| cried | feet | tea | really | he's |
| keep | morning | top | wind | river |
| room | queen | eyes | wish | liked |
| last | each | fell | eggs | giant |
| jumped | book | friends | once | looks |
| because | its | box | please | use |
| even | green | dark | thing | along |
| am | different | grandad | stopped | plants |
| before | let | there's | ever | dragon |
| gran | girl | looking | miss | pulled |
| clothes | which | end | most | we're |
| tell | inside | than | cold | fly |
| key | run | best | park | grow |

# Stories about my world

## Objectives Overview

| Learning Objective | Objective Code | Learner's book Activities | Teacher's pack Activities | Workbook Activities |
|---|---|---|---|---|
| **Reading** | | | | |
| Hear, read and write initial letter sounds. | 1R01 | 6 | 13, 15 | 2 |
| Identify separate sounds (phonemes) within words, which may be represented by more than one letter, e.g. 'th', 'ch', 'sh'. | 1R03 | 7 | 15, 17 | 3 |
| Use knowledge of sounds to read and write single syllable words with short vowels. | 1R04 | 9 | 21 | |
| Use phonic knowledge to read decodable words and to attempt to sound out some elements of unfamiliar words. | 1R06 | 14 | 21 | |
| Demonstrate an understanding that one spoken word corresponds with one written word. | 1R07 | 4, 16 | 13, 25 | |
| Join in with reading familiar, simple stories and poems. | 1R08 | 4, 16 | 13, 25 | |
| Know that in English, print is read from left to right and top to bottom. | 1R09 | 4 | 13 | |
| Read a range of common words on sight. | 1R10 | 14 | 21 | 7 |
| Make links to own experiences. | 1R12 | 15 | 23 | |
| Retell stories, with some appropriate use of story language. | 1R13 | 19 | 25 | |
| Read aloud independently from simple books. | 1R16 | 11 | 20 | |
| Pause at full stops when reading. | 1R17 | 10 | 19 | |
| Identify sentences in a text. | 1R18 | 10 | 19 | |
| Anticipate what happens next in a story. | 1Ri1 | 17 | 25 | |
| Talk about events in a story and make simple inferences about characters and events to show understanding. | 1Ri2 | 8, 14, 18 | 17, 21, 25 | 8 |
| Recognise story elements, e.g. beginning, middle and end. | 1Rw2 | 8 | 17 | |
| **Writing** | | | | |
| Form letters correctly. | 1W02 | 9 | 17 | 5 |
| Know that a capital letter is used for *I*, for proper nouns and for the start of a sentence. | 1W03 | 10 | 19 | |
| Use knowledge of sounds to write simple regular words, and to attempt other words including when writing simple sentences dictated by the teacher from memory. | 1W04 | | 17 | 4 |
| Write simple storybooks with sentences to caption pictures. | 1Wa1 | 21 | 27 | |
| Write for a purpose using some basic features of text type. | 1Wa5 | 24 | | |
| Compose and write a simple sentence with a capital letter and a full stop. | 1Wp2 | 11 | 19 | 6 |
| **Speaking and listening** | | | | |
| Speak clearly and choose words carefully to express feelings and ideas when speaking of matters of immediate interest. | 1SL1 | 8, 15 | 23, 24 | |
| Show some awareness of the listener through non-verbal communication. | 1SL3 | 20 | 27 | |

# The dragon in the hall

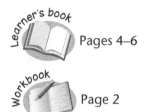

Learner's book

Pages 4–6

Workbook

Page 2

## Objectives

- Demonstrate an understanding that one spoken word corresponds with one written word. (1R07)
- Join in with reading familiar, simple stories and poems. (1R08)
- Know that in English, print is read from left to right and top to bottom. (1R09)
- Hear, read and write initial letter sounds. (1R01)

## Starter

- Explain to the learners that they are going to read a story. Ask: *What is a story?* Let partners give an answer to each other before you accept any answers. Agree that a story is made up.
- Talk about story settings. Ask: *Where do stories take place?* Agree that the setting can be anywhere. They are often ordinary places that the readers will recognise from their own lives.
- Show the learners a range of stories, making sure that they all have settings that the learners may find familiar. For each, discuss the cover and read aloud the blurb on the back. Ask: *Where do you think this story is set? Is that an unusual place? Is it like a place that you know?* Share experiences.
- Direct the learners to page 4 of their Learner's book. Read aloud the name of the story. In what ordinary place do the learners think this story will be set? (In a house.)
- Read the first part of the story on page 4. Pause and ask: *What do you think will happen next?* Use talk partners for the children to exchange ideas. Widen the discussion to share results as a class.
- Finish the story. Did any of the children correctly predict the ending? Ask: *How did Sonja feel by the end?* (She did not have to be frightened.)
- Read the text again, slowly, so that the learners can follow with their fingers. Watch to see that they are pointing to one word at a time. Afterwards ask the learners to use a head movement to show you the direction in which their finger has been travelling. When you were reading aloud, did their eyes and finger move down the page?

## Activity notes and answers

1. **Listen to reading of story.** Model pointing to each word as you read.

# Starting phonemes

1. **Recognise initial phonemes in words.** Remind the learners that words are made up of sounds (phonemes). Say these four words for them to repeat after you: bad, cat, hot, sit. Do this again, this time the children repeating just the first sound in each word: *b, k, h, s.* Write on the board: bad, cat, hot, sit. Enlist the learners' help in reading the words aloud, and underline the letter in each word making the initial sound: <u>b</u>ad, <u>c</u>at, <u>h</u>ot, <u>s</u>it.

   Direct the learners to activity 1 on page 6 of the Learner's book. Working in pairs, let the learners say the words represented by the pictures. Can they hear the initial sound for each? Say the sound for them to copy. Write each one, one at a time, on the board. Demonstrate individual letter formation for them to copy the word. Encourage them to help each other to write the word.

   **Answers:** a) c     b) h     c) b     d) s

2. **Identify words that start with the same phoneme.** Read the words from the cloud on page 6 of the Learner's book as the learners follow. Read them again with the learners joining in. Explain that the words need sorting into pairs and that each pair must start with the same phoneme. Read the first word aloud.

Ask them for a sign, for example, hand in the air, when you read the word starting with the same sound. Partners could read aloud for each other.

**Answers:** nip, nut; map, mum; pin, pip; leg, lot

3. **Find words from the story that start with particular phonemes.** Direct the learners to pages 4 and 5 of their Learner's book. Read the text again, slowly, so that the learners can follow with their fingers. Watch to see that they are pointing to one word at a time. Afterwards ask the learners to point a finger to show you the direction in which their finger has been travelling. When you were reading aloud, did their eyes and finger move down the page?

Ask them to find a word in the story, starting with the phonemes shown in activity 3. Let partners help each other to search the text.

**Possible answers:**

b  baby, back, but

h  hall, here

r  ran

## Workbook answers

**Starting phonemes**

**Answers:**

1. a) doll – drum
   b) end – egg
   c) friend – frog
   d) goat – girl
   e) cap – cake
   f) teddy – tent

2. a) <u>j</u>ug
   b) <u>ch</u>eek
   c) <u>w</u>as
   d) <u>sh</u>ut

## Success criteria ✔

While completing the activities, assess and record learners who can:

- follow a line of text from left to right
- understand that text moves from top to bottom
- recognise that one spoken word corresponds with one written word
- hear, read and write initial letter sounds.

**IT** Create a pdf of a short section of the story (Learner's book pages 4–5) and load it onto your computer. Remove some familiar high frequency words and common words. When the learners are following your reading with their finger, you pause because you reach an empty place in your text; can the children find the word in the line of their Learner's book? Can they tell you what to type in a note box for the empty place?

## Further activities

- Create word cards using some of the high frequency words that are used in 'The dragon in the hall' (Learner's book pages 4–5). Ask partners to take turns reading the cards to each other. Challenge the listening partner to find the word in the story.
- Ask learners to think of another ordinary place for a story about Sonja and her family. Let them use a three-picture storyboard to tell their story.
- Ask learners to complete Workbook page 2.
- Read the learners the story listed in the Book list below about a girl at school.

## Book list

- *Amazing Grace*, by Mary Hoffman (France Lincoln Children's Books)

# Sh

Page 7

Page 3

Learner's book Page 7

Workbook Page 3

## Objectives

- Hear, read and write initial sounds. (1R01)
- Identify separate sounds (phonemes) within words, which may be represented by more than one letter, e.g. 'th', 'ch', 'sh'. (1R03)

## Starter

- Hold up the letters *sh*. Put your finger to your lips, as if you want the learners to be quiet. Ask: *Can you work out what sound I am making?* (*sh*) Repeat the sound for the learners to repeat after you. Encourage them to make the action and repeat the sound to a partner. Draw pictures or identify images or objects in the room where the *sh* phoneme is made by these two letters. For example: ship, dish, brush, shop, shelf, hush. Ask learners to say the words and identify if the *sh* sound starts or finishes the word.

## Activity notes and answers

**Helpful hints:** Direct the learners to the Helpful hints box on page 7 of the Learner's book. Invite them to imitate the action in the picture and to make the new sound aloud. Ask them to read aloud the words (shop, wish). Can they see the written sound (grapheme)? How is one word different from the other? (One word begins with the new sound, one ends with it.) When they listen to the words read aloud, can they hear where the *sh* sound is?

1. **Name objects from pictures.** Point out the pictures in question 1 on Learner's book page 7 and agree what the images are. Explain that some begin with an *s* sound, some begin with *sh*. Can the learners sort the pictures into two groups? Suggest that they write **s** next to one group of pictures and **sh** next to other pictures.

   **Answers:**

   **s** sea, sack, six

   **sh** shell, shoe, shark

2. **Find phonemes in the story.** Return to the story on pages 4–5 of the Learner's book. Explain that while you read the story aloud, the children should follow the words, listening for two words in the story that begin with the *sh* phoneme. Ask the learners to find and write those words. Read the story again as the learners listen, recognise and copy two words starting with the *sh* phoneme and two starting with the *s* phoneme.

   **Answers:**

   she, shush

   Sonja, silly

## Success criteria ✓

While completing the activities, assess and record learners who can:

- hear, read and write initial sounds
- understand that two letters can work together to make a new phoneme
- recognise separate sounds within words.

## Workbook answers

**sh or s**

**s** phoneme: sit, miss, bus, hiss, silly

**sh** phoneme: ship, cash, shop, rush, shut

neither phoneme: bat, hut, tip, chin, pot, hat

## Further activities

- Ask the learners, in pairs, to think of two or three words starting with a *sh* sound and using the grapheme (written letters) 'sh'. Ask them to draw images. Can they write the words?
- Ask learners to complete Workbook page 3.

## Assessment ideas

- Use a suitable fiction text that contains words using 'sh'. Read the text aloud, inviting the learners to put a finger to their lips when they hear *sh*. Show the learners the text and read it aloud again. Can the learners find and write the words?

# Beginning, middle and end

Pages 8–9

Pages 4–5

## Objectives

- Recognise story elements, e.g. beginning, middle and end. (1RW2)
- Use knowledge of sounds to write simple regular words, and to attempt other words including when writing simple sentences dictated by the teacher from memory. (1W04)
- Identify separate sounds (phonemes) within words, which may be represented by more than one letter, e.g. 'th', 'ch', 'sh'. (1R03)
- Form letters correctly. (1W02)

## Starter

- Return to pages 4 and 5 of the Learner's book and read aloud the title 'The dragon in the hall' and the two pages of text. Ask: *What sort of writing is on these two pages?* (A story.) What do the learners understand by the word 'story'? Agree that a story is in a place (setting); is usually about people or animals or things (characters); and something happen (events).
- Discuss 'The dragon in the hall': where it is set; who it is about; and what happens. Talk about how it begins, what happens in the middle; how it ends.
- Point out that this story does not suddenly stop: it comes to a sensible end. Ask: *Do you think this is important?* Suggest that otherwise the reader would be left wondering what would happen.
- Direct the learners to page 8 of the Learner's book. Point to and read aloud the terms, **Beginning**, **The Middle** and **End**. Read the explanation next to each term. Suggest that this story has those parts. Return to pages 4 and 5 and read the story aloud again. Hold group and then whole class discussions about which parts of the pages form each section. Which section is the longest? (The middle.)

## Activity notes and answers

1. **Label the story parts.** Direct the learners to page 8 of the Learner's book. Read aloud the three sentences about Sonja. Ask the learners to put them in their story order by writing 'Beginning', 'Middle' or 'End' next to the sentences they have copied into their books. You may prefer to support some learners by providing a worksheet on which you have already typed the sentences.

   **Answers:**
   a) Sonja tells her mother that there are no monsters. **End**
   b) Sonja is in bed. **Beginning**
   c) Sonja comforts the baby when she cries. **Middle**

2. **Understand a story.** Point out the words 'true' and 'false'. Read and explain their meanings: correct and incorrect. As the learners follow, read aloud each sentence in turn. Offer relevant prompts about the story (for example, with sentence c, Sonja went to comfort her sister) and let partners talk to each other before they write true or false.

**Talk about being scared.** Be ready to provide adult support to some learners, perhaps with sentence openers (One time I felt scared when …). Ask them if they can offer each other tips for feeling braver.

# Writing *sh* and *ch*

## Activity notes and answers

**Helpful hints:** Direct the learners to the Helpful hints box on page 9 of the Learner's book. Say the word *chop*, emphasising the initial sound *ch* for the learners to repeat.

**Writing presentation: Practise *sh* and *ch*.** Have your back to the class as learners copy your letter formation in the air. Remind learners about pencil grip and start and finish points of these letters.

1. **Learners recognise the sounds.** Look at the images on page 9 together. Can the learners say a word for each picture? As a class, say the words aloud. Ask them to listen as you say the words. What two sounds do they notice? (*sh, ch*) Write the words on the board for the children to copy under the correct picture. Ask them to underline 'sh' or 'ch' in each.

   **Answers:** a) chick    b) fish    c) ship    d) shop    e) chin

### Success criteria

While completing the activities, assess and record learners who can:

- recognise story elements, e.g. beginning, middle and end
- hear, read and write initial sounds
- recognise separate sounds within words
- understand that two letters can work together to make a new phoneme
- form letters correctly.

### Workbook answers

**Short words**

- mum, sum, sun, fun
- fan, man
- mat, pat

 Use a computer to create three boxes. Use a design package to put an image for parts of a story in each box. Type three sentences about the story in another place on the page. Ask the learners to match the sentences to the boxes, cutting and pasting them. Can they put the labels 'Beginning', 'Middle' and 'End' with the correct box and sentence? Can they move the boxes into the story's correct order?

## Further activities

- Put the learners into pairs with two cards: one card should say 'true', the other 'false'. Play a game in which you make new statements about the story, 'The dragon in the hall'. Allow time for partner discussion before partners decide which card to hold up.
- Demonstrate an efficient pencil grip. Check the grip of individual learners and make corrections.
- Ask learners to complete Workbook pages 4–5.

### Assessment ideas

- Provide the learners with images, in random order, of these words: *chocolate, wash, shell, chop, cheese, shoe.* Show and read the words aloud. Ask learners to match the words to the pictures and to underline the letters making the *sh* or *ch* sound.

# Grammar and punctuation

Learner's book Pages 10–11

Workbook Page 6

## Objectives

- Pause at full stops when reading. (1R17)
- Identify sentences in a text. (1R18)
- Compose and write a simple sentence with a capital letter and a full stop. (1Wp2)
- Know that a capital letter is used for *I*, for proper nouns and for the start of a sentence. (1W03)

## Starter

- Write this simple paragraph on the board for the learners to look at:

  *Sonja was a big girl now. She was much too big for a cot. She was too big for her little bed. Her mother got her a new bed. At first Sonja did not like this bed.*

- Explain that you have put the words into groups. Each group is called a sentence. Ask: *When you look at the writing, can you tell where a sentence starts and ends?* (There are full stops.)

- Explain that a sentence is a group of words that makes sense. Give the learners this example:
  *Her mother got* is not a sentence.
  *Her mother got her a new bed.* is a sentence.

- Read the paragraph aloud to the learners. What do they notice about your voice? Read it again if necessary, prompting them to recognise your pauses between sentences.

**Helpful hints:** Read the definition of a sentence on page 10 of the Learner's book aloud. Check with the learners that you have put a capital letter at the beginning and a full stop at the end of each sentence on the whiteboard.

Direct the learners to the cartoon shark on page 10 of the Learner's book. Read aloud the sentence as the learners follow the words. Ask: *How many sentences are there?* (One.) Invite partners to point out the capital letter and full stop to each other.

## Activity notes and answers

1. **Count sentences.** If needed, read the story aloud as the learners follow. Ask them to watch out for capital letters and full stops. Let partners take turns reading the story to each other. Encourage them to check with each other how many sentences they have counted. They should check again before writing down their answers.

   **Answer:** Four sentences.

2. **Recognise sentences.** Remind the learners that a group of words can only be a sentence if it makes sense. Put the learners into pairs to read the groups of words to each other. Ask them to write 'sentence' for the groups that make sentences, and 'no' for the other groups. Did anything else help them to decide?

   **Answers:** a and d are sentences.

**Workbook answers**

**Cool in the pool**

a) We are sent to bed.

b) The pool is cool.

c) The sun is hot.

d) Dad is cross with us.

## More sentences

**Read and listen to the story.** Remind the learners to make sure their voice helps their listening partner – they need to pause at the full stops. Listeners should be ready to advise their talk partner how to do better.

1. **Complete sentences.** Remind the learners about recognising a sentence. Ask: *What is at the beginning? What is at the end?* Read aloud the sentences in activity 1 as the learners follow. Ask them to write them out correctly.

   **Answers:**

   a) My mum has a green dress.

   b) I have lost my book.

   c) The ball has gone over the wall.

   d) The children will help.

**Try this:** Point out that the learners can use words in the pictures to help them. Remind them that their finished sentence must make sense. Reading the sentence aloud will help them check.

**Example answers:**

a) There is a frog on the log.

b) The shop is shut.

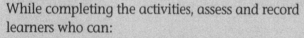

### Success criteria

While completing the activities, assess and record learners who can:

- pause at full stops when reading
- identify sentences in a text
- put in missing capital letters and full stops
- write an ending to sentences.

### Further activities

- Ask the learners to return to *Try this!* and to finish the sentences in new ways.
- Suggest the learners challenge their partner to find what is missing (a capital letter or full stop). They must write three sentences, each with one or two things missing. Can their partner point out what needs to change so they are correct sentences?
- Write a collection of complete and incomplete sentences. Can the learners identify which is which? Invite them to complete your unfinished sentences.
- Ask learners to complete Workbook page 6.

# Reading fiction

Learner's book
Pages 12–14

Workbook
Page 7

## Objectives

- Read a range of common words on sight. (1R10)
- Use phonic knowledge to read decodable words and to attempt to sound out some elements of unfamiliar words. (1R06)

## Starter

- Ask the learners to explain to their partner what a story is. (It is not true.) Agree that it is a made-up piece of writing. Explain that 'fiction' is another word for a story or made-up writing.
- Show the difference between fiction and truth with these two texts:
  a) Children work in this room.
  b) Red monkeys and blue tigers read books in this room.
  Can the learners tell which is which? How? (a) tells the truth; b) is impossible fiction.)
- Point out that fiction, because it is made up, is often not serious. Writers may choose a word just because they like the sound of it.
- Direct the learners to pages 12 and 13 of the Learner's book. Read pages 12 and 13 aloud as the learners follow. Ask: *Do you think this is fiction (a story) or truth? Why do you think that?* (The learners should be aware of the talking animals.)
- Read the story aloud again as the learners follow. This time, pause before rhyming words. Can learners help you say the next word? (The writer's deliberate choice of funny rhyming words helps.) Point out the rhymes and explain that rhymes are words that end with the same sound. Point out 'zoo' in the first line of the story. Say the long *oo* for the learners to repeat. Read the story again, learners repeating the word when they hear the *oo* sound.

## Activity notes and answers

**Helpful hints:** Point out the Helpful hints box on page 13 of the Learner's book. If the learners break these difficult words up into letter patterns, does that help them to read the words?

# Lost at the zoo

1. **Read and write common words.** Show the learners the list of words on page 14. Put the learners into pairs to read the words to each other. Check that everyone is reading them correctly before they look for the words in the story on Learner's book pages 12–13. Demonstrate on the board how to form the letters. Encourage the learners to practise drawing the letter shapes with a finger before they write.

2. **Answer questions about the story.** Put the learners into small discussion groups. Read pages 12–13 aloud as the learners follow the story. Ask them to discuss what happens in the story. Prompt discussion with questions: *Who is the story about? Where do they go? What happens while they are there? Is there a happy ending?*

   Point out the questions in activity 2. Explain that the learners have to choose the correct answer for each. Encourage group members to read questions aloud, talk about them, find and check that part of the story on pages 12–13, and decide on their answer.

   **Answers:** a) Blue Kangaroo    b) A parrot    c) The monkeys    d) With the kangaroos

## Success criteria ✓

While completing the activities, assess and record learners who can:

- use phonic knowledge to read decodable words and to attempt to sound out some elements of unfamiliar words
- read a range of common words on sight.

**IT** Prepare a document on a computer for the learners to use. Have a number of animal names, but always with a vowel missing. List the letters that the learners can choose from: *i, o, a*. They must type in the missing letter. Learners could add a picture from Clipart. Suggested animals include: cat, dog, fish, fox, frog.

## Further activities

- Give the learners this list of common words: *were, at, up, he, and, the, with*. As with activity 1 on page 14 of the Learner's book, they must find the words in the story, and practise reading and writing them.
- Ask the learners to pick out words in the story that they do not understand. Suggest they share results with a partner. Does their partner know the meaning? Can they work it out from what is happening in the story? Have they checked the Glossary?
- Return to some unfamiliar words from the previous activity. Does the spelling help them work out how to say the words?
- Ask learners to play the game on Workbook page 7.
- Read some other stories about Blue Kangaroo to the class (see Book list below).

## Assessment ideas

- Reuse the story from Learner's book pages 12–13, but omit some common or decodable words. Place the words in a box at the bottom of the page. Ask the learners to place the words correctly.

## Book list

Other stories about Blue Kangaroo by Emma Chichester Clark (HarperCollins Children's books):

- *What Shall We Do, Blue Kangaroo?*
- *Happy Birthday, Blue Kangaroo!*
- *Come to School Too, Blue Kangaroo!*

# Feelings

 Page 15

 Page 8

**Objectives**

- Make links to own experiences. (1R12)
- Speak clearly and choose words carefully to express feelings and ideas when speaking of matters of immediate interest. (1SL1)

## Starter

- Remind the learners that a story is about made-up happenings. Suggest that even though fiction (a story) is not true, it can still be like real life.

- Explain that stories can sometimes remind us of our own lives. Give an example from a classroom story you have read or listened to together. Discuss similarities to the learners' lives. (For example, the story may be set in a similar place or the characters may have similar things happening to them.)

- Read the story on Learner's book pages 12–13 as the learners follow. Discuss what happens in the story. Ask: *Who are the main characters?* (Blue Kangaroo and Lily.) *Where do they go?* (The zoo.) *What worrying thing happens while they are there?* (Blue Kangaroo gets lost.) *Does everything turn out well?* (Yes.)

- Put the learners into pairs, one taking the part of Lily, one acting as Blue Kangaroo. As you read page 13 aloud, the learners should act their parts. Afterwards, invite partners to tell each other how they felt. Change roles and do the reading, acting and talking again.

## Activity notes and answers

1. **Read and write.** Read activity 1 on Learner's book page 15 to the learners. Ask them to think about how they felt when they were pretending to be Lily. Point out the words 'worried' and 'happy'. They must write one of the words after each statement.

   **Answers:**
   a) worried
   b) happy

**Talk Partners**

**Think about a time when you lost something.** Ask the learners to think about when they lost something that was special to them, for example a toy, a book, a photograph. Allow time for them to think about how they felt when they could not find it. Put the learners into pairs to do this talking and listening exercise. Suggest that they tell a partner about what happened and how they felt. Remind them of the need to look at their partner, speak clearly and listen carefully. Ask: *Where should the listening partner look? Should they listen carefully?*

**Workbook answers**

**Lost!**
a) happy
b) bored
c) worried
d) happy

2. **Express feelings.** Direct the learners to activity 2 on page 15 of the Learner's book. Remind them of their conversation with their partner. Read aloud the instructions as the children follow. Suggest that their pictures should show their feelings as well as what happened. When the learners are writing their sentences, provide adult support so that, when necessary, words can be written for them to copy.

   **Example answers:**

   I lost my teddy when I was in the park.

   When I lost my teddy I felt sad.

### Success criteria

While completing the activities, assess and record learners who can:

- talk about their own experiences
- speak clearly and choose words carefully when talking about their own experiences.

### Further activities

- Reminding themselves of what they lost, the learners should use activity 2, on Learner's book page 15, as a model. Ask them to draw pictures and write sentences about where they found what they had lost, and how they felt.

- Ask the learners to reread 'Lily and Blue Kangaroo at the Zoo' from Learner's book pages 12–13. Ask: *What could the monkeys be doing that was naughty? How do you think the lions seemed haughty? Which animal would you be? What would you do?* Ask talk partners to tell each other how they would behave.

- Put learners in pairs to tell each other about a visit they made to a zoo or a place with animals. What did they most enjoy? Why? Encourage eye contact, clear speech and careful listening as partners talk to each other.

- Ask learners to complete Workbook page 8.

# Five Minutes' Peace

Pages 16–19

## Objectives

- Demonstrate an understanding that one spoken word corresponds with one written word. (1R07)
- Join in with reading familiar, simple stories and poems. (1R08)
- Anticipate what happens next in a story. (1Ri1)
- Talk about events in a story and make simple inferences about characters and events to show understanding. (1Ri2)
- Retell stories with some appropriate use of story language. (1R13)

## Starter

- Introduce the word 'character'. Explain that the characters are who a story is about.
- Show the learners some storybooks from the classroom that all have animal characters. Ask: *Which of these stories have you read? Did you like them? Why? Did the animals seem like people?*
- Ask the learners to bring a storybook – that they have enjoyed – from home and show it to a partner. Can they tell their partner what happens in the story?
- Compare the books chosen by the learners. Ask: *Whose story had animals in it?* Suggest that animals are popular characters in children's stories. *Why?* Suggest that it may be because they can often seem like us.
- Point out that even when stories have animal characters, the stories can still remind us of things that happen in our lives. Is this because the story animals talk and behave like people?

## Activity notes and answers

1. **Read the story.** Direct the learners to Learner's book pages 16–17 and read the story aloud as they follow. Point out and question the learners about the important details in the illustrations. Ask: *Are the young elephants eating politely? Does Mrs Large's tray look more pleasant? Are Mrs Large's children leaving her alone?*

   Reread the story, this time with the learners' help in reading some parts. Be ready to help them with those parts – or repeat them – until the learners gain the confidence to read some short lines independently. Divide the story in this way: the learners read the title and first sentence; you read the rest of page 16; the learners reread page 16.

2. **Learners say what will happen next.** Discuss as a class what happens in the story. Put the learners into pairs to talk about what may happen next. Make sure that each partner has the chance and confidence to speak. When you share some of these ideas as a class, emphasise that there is no correct answer.

# Who and where

1. **Answer questions.** Ask the learners to follow as you read aloud the questions on page 18 of the Learner's book. Ask: *What does 'character' mean? What is a setting?* Point out the Helpful hints box and read aloud the word definitions. Suggest that pictures as well as words in the story will help them find the answers. Reread the questions and put the learners into pairs to help each other. Provide these sentence starters for writing the answers:
   a) The characters are …
   b) The story is set in …
   c) The children are …
   d) Mrs Large is going to …
   e) She wants …

**Answers:**

a) The characters are the Large family.
b) The story is set in the house.
c) The children are having breakfast.
d) Mrs Large is going to the bathroom.
e) She wants five minutes' peace.

## Retelling a story

1. **Tell a story.** Point out the story map on page 19 of the Learner's book. Suggest that the writer has made this plan before writing the story. It is a plan of what will happen and the illustrations. Read the caption for image 5. What does this tell us about Mrs Large's hopes? (She will never get any peace.) Put the learners into pairs and remind them to talk clearly as they use the map to tell the story to their partner.

**Talk Partners** **Discuss how Mrs Large and the children feel.** Suggest partners look together at the picture of Mrs Large and the children in the bathroom. Do the characters' faces help the learners decide how the characters feel? What do both partners think?

**Success criteria** ✓

While completing the activities, assess and record learners who can:

- join in with reading the story
- say what they think will happen next in the story
- answer questions about the characters, setting and story
- use the story map to retell the story.

**IT** The site *www.tes.co.uk/ teaching-resources* has resources with differentiated comprehension questions based on this book for guided reading/writing sessions.

### Further activities

- Organise reading groups, each group with a book of a suitable reading level. Provide adult support for the group to join in reading some parts aloud.
- Read a new story to the learners. Choose one that has a familiar setting and animal characters. Let learners talk to a partner about what may happen next. Share ideas in a class discussion.
- Read the learners more stories about the Large family (see Book list below).

### Assessment ideas

- Listen in to the *Tell a story* activity. Assess the children's ability to talk about the events of a story; the appropriateness of their language; their speaking and listening skills.

**Book list**

- *A Quiet Night In* and other books about the Large family by Jill Murphy (Walker Books)

# Peace and quiet

Pages 20–21

Page 9

**Objectives**

- Show some awareness of the listener through non-verbal communication. (1SL3)
- Write simple storybooks with sentences to caption pictures. (1Wa1)

## Starter

- Tell the learners that you are going to talk to them about something. For example, arranging the classroom books and furniture. Ask them to see what they notice about your face and body while you talk.

- Involve another adult to tell you their views about the arrangement of the classroom. Emphasise to the learners that you want them to still keep noticing how you behave while you are listening.

- Let partners share observations before you share findings as a class. Did the listeners notice where you looked, what direction you faced, if you had an interested expression on your face? Explain that these are all important when we speak or listen to someone.

- Remind the learners about the story *Five Minutes' Peace*. Talk about when you like peace and being away from noise and other people. Ask: *Do you ever want peace and quiet?* Invite learners to share their answers.

## Activity notes and answers

1. **Draw pictures for a story.** Direct the learners to Learner's book page 20. Question the learners about each picture: what is happening, what the boy may be thinking, what he would like to do. Point out that in each picture the boy is being disturbed by the noise of one of his family. What does the boy always want? (Some peace.) Draw attention to the final picture. What has happened? (The boy has found some peace to read his book by going out in the rain.)

   Read aloud the instructions for activity 1. Suggest the learners draw three or four pictures for their new story about the boy wanting peace. Let them use a book format, with a new page for every picture.

**Talk Partners**

**Partners listen to each other's stories.** Suggest that the learners first look at their pictures and tell themselves the story. They can say the words in their heads or aloud quietly to themselves before they tell the story to a partner. Remind both partners of the need to take turns speaking, to listen to each other, and to make eye contact.

# Writing captions

1. Introduce the learners to the word *caption*. Do the learners know what it means? Explain that it is a line of writing – a sentence or just some words – written under a picture. The caption makes what is happening in the picture easier to understand. Look together at the four pictures in activity 1 on Learner's book page 20. Work with the learners to think of captions. Write them on the board.

   **Example answers**

   a) The TV was too loud.

   b) His brother made such a noise.

   c) His sister and her friends were cooking again.

   d) Now he had some peace.

   Read the instruction at the top of Learner's book page 21 to the learners. Talk about working out their caption; saying it to themselves; writing it. Remind them to use the checklist to help them write their words. Point out the Helpful hints box and read through the What have I learnt? checklist with the children. Remind them that *phonics* means putting sounds together.

---

**Success criteria**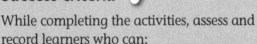

While completing the activities, assess and record learners who can:

- listen carefully to their partner's story
- write simple captions for their pictures.

IT

Suggest that the learners transfer their story to a computer. The finished product could look like a book. Use a story-writing package to allow the learners to create their own books. 'We are writers' is available on *http://writers.scholastic.co.uk.*

---

**Further activities**

- Learners complete the Self-assessment table on page 9 of the Workbook.
- Hold partner conversations about how the learners think their classroom should be arranged. Does it need a book corner? Should there be quiet area to give people some peace?
- Create groups of four so that partners can watch and listen to another pair having a conversation. Afterwards they can give one another constructive feedback about their speaking and listening skills.

# Unit 2 Signs, labels and instructions

## Objectives Overview

| Learning Objective | Objective Code | Learner's book Activities | Teacher's pack Activities | Workbook Activities |
|---|---|---|---|---|
| **Reading** | | | | |
| Know the name of and most common sound associated with every letter in the English alphabet. | 1R02 | 27 | 34 | |
| Identify separate sounds (phonemes) within words, which may be represented by more than one letter, e.g. 'th', 'ch', 'sh'. | 1R03 | 27, 31, 37 | 34, 42 | 12 |
| Use knowledge of sounds to read and write single syllable words with short vowels. | 1R04 | 26, 29 | 34 | |
| Use phonic knowledge to read decodable words and to attempt to sound out some elements of unfamiliar words. | 1R06 | 34, 35 | 40 | |
| Read a range of common words on sight. | 1R10 | 28, 29, 31, 32 | 36, 37, 38 | |
| Read labels, lists and captions to find information. | 1Rx1 | 22, 23, 24, 36 | 30, 40 | 10 |
| Show awareness that texts for different purposes look different, e.g. use of photographs, diagrams. | 1Rv1 | 26, 30 | 34, 36 | 13 |
| **Writing** | | | | |
| Form letters correctly. | 1W02 | 33 | 38 | 15 |
| Write for a purpose using some basic features of text type. | 1Wa5 | 24, 39 | 30, 44 | 11, 16 |
| Write simple information texts with labels, captions, lists, questions and instructions for a purpose. | 1Wa6 | 39 | 44 | 16 |
| Write sentence-like structures which may be joined by *and*. | 1Wp3 | 31, 32, 33 | 38, 39 | 14 |
| **Speaking and listening** | | | | |
| Converse audibly with friends, teachers and other adults. | 1SL2 | 25, 38 | 33, 44 | |
| Listen carefully to questions and instructions. | 1SL8 | 36 | 40 | |
| Engage in imaginative play, enacting simple characters or situations. | 1SL9 | 25 | 33 | |

# Signs

Learner's book
Pages 22–24

Workbook
Pages 10–11

**Objectives**

- Read labels, lists and captions to find information. (1Rx1)
- Write for a purpose using some basic features of text type. (1Wa5)

## Starter

- Point to and read aloud the heading of this unit. Explain that signs, labels and instructions are all sets of words that help people. They provide important information.

- Show the learners an item of clothing with a label inside. Can they guess what information is on this label? (It tells you the size of the garment, its material and how to look after it.) Do any of the learners have a bag with a label inside? Is there a picture on the classroom wall with a name label underneath?

- Ask the learners to think about your school. Is there a *sign* outside? What does it tell people? (Perhaps the name of the school or that children are crossing.)

- Ask: *What are instructions?* (They tell people to do something, or not to do it.) Can the children think of instructions on display inside or outside your school? Prompt the learners with references to an instruction perhaps near the grass in front of your school, or about which door to use or where to park.

- Give other examples by saying these two instructions to the learners: *Stand up. Face the back of the room.* Did all the learners obey?

- Give these oral instructions: *Don't have your feet on the floor. Don't cross your arms.* Did everyone obey? Ask: *What was different about the second two instructions?* (They told the learners *not* to do something.)

- Direct the learners to Learner's book pages 22–23. Ask: *What is this place?* (A pet shop.) *What are the pieces of writing on the cages or walls?* (Signs and instructions.) *Why do you think the writing is important?* (People may need special information about being near these animals.)

## Activity notes and answers

1. **Read the signs.** Put the learners into pairs to help each other find the correct sign as you read it aloud. Then direct the learners to places on the pages and read the signs together. Finally, support just one pair of readers in reading a sign with you.

2. **Finding signs.** Make sure that there is a variety of signs on display in the classroom. Explain to the learners that some of the signs are labels (they may say what is in that place), and some are instructions (they give a command). Put the learners into small groups to wander around the room. They should copy the writing on the sign they see and make a quick sketch of where it is. Give every group an opportunity to read and show some of their findings. Are there any signs they have missed?

**Helpful hints:** point out the Helpful hints on Learner's book page 23 and read the box together. Invite the learners to give you their own examples for each type of instruction.

# Bossy words

**Helpful hints:** Read the Helpful hints box on Learner's book page 24 to the learners. Ask: *What does a command do?* (It tells you to do something.)

1.  **Find command words.** Explain that all these command (bossy) words are in the signs in the pet shop on pages 22 and 23. Read the words aloud to the learners. Can they read them again without you? Suggest that the children copy the signs containing the words when they find them in the pet shop.

    **Answers:**

    | | | |
    |---|---|---|
    | Take care: I bite | Don't feed me. | Talk to me. |
    | Stroke me. | Shush: don't shout. | Do not run. |
    | Pay here. | Don't tap the glass. | Push. |

2.  **Recognise and write command words.** Read the sentences with the learners. Put the learners into pairs to read the sentences to each other. This will help them to identify the command words.

    **Answers:**
    a) Pop
    b) Cut
    c) Put
    d) Sit
    e) Try

**Success criteria**

While completing the activities, assess and record learners who can:

*   read labels, lists and captions to find information
*   write imperative verbs ('bossy words').

**IT** Use the animal safari park poster and its interactive game on instructions at *www.scholastic.co.uk*. The children will have fun as they learn when deciding which animal gives which command.

**Workbook answers**

**Signs around us**
1.  a) on a road
    b) near a school
    c) on the school front door
    d) on a door
    e) on a recycling bin for glass

**Bossy words**
1.  a) Race
    b) Run
    c) Fold

2.  a) Drink
    b) Wash
    c) Chop
    d) Post

## Further activities

*   Learner's complete Workbook pages 10–11.
*   Ask the learners to return to activity 1 on page 24 of the Learner's book. Put them into small groups. Group members should take turns reading a sign aloud. The other members must pretend to be people in the pet shop. How will they behave to show they understand the sign?
*   Suggest the learners draw a picture of a person. They need three speech bubbles coming from the mouth. In each bubble, the learners must write a command sentence that the person is saying.
*   Put the learners into pairs or small groups to play a game of giving and receiving instructions. They must be commands that can be done in the classroom.

## Assessment ideas

Give the learners these written instructions. Read them to the learners before you ask them to find and write the command words:

- Stay away from here.
- Talk quietly.
- Put your bag down.
- Close the door.
- Lock the cage.
- Watch for spiders.
- Take no photographs.
- Eat outside.

**Answers:**

Stay

Talk

Put

Close

Lock

Watch

Take

Eat

# Role play

Page 25

Learner's book

## Objectives

● Engage in imaginative play, enacting simple characters or situations. (1SL9)

● Converse audibly with friends, teachers and other adults. (1SL2)

## Starter

● Ask: *What is an instruction?* (Sentences telling people to do or not do something.) *What sort of word is used in an instruction?* (A bossy word.)

● Suggest that shopkeepers often give instructions to their customers.

● Direct the learners to Learner's book pages 22–23. Ask: *What type of shop is this? Have you ever been in a pet shop?*

● Share experiences. Suggest that this shopkeeper will give instructions about an animal's care; food and water; touching and stroking; the use of a cage.

● Ask: W*hat type of words will the shopkeeper keep using?* (Bossy words.) Ask the learners for examples of instructions this shopkeeper might give. (*Wait here. Look at that snake. Watch his tongue.*)

## Activity notes and answers

**Talk Partners**

**Play pet shops.** Read the Talk Partners box on Learner's book page 25 to the learners. Put the learners into pairs to take the roles. Remind the 'shopkeeper' to use bossy words and to speak clearly. Repeat the activity with the learners in the other role.

1. **Understand bossy words.** Agree with the learners what action each picture shows. Write on the board a bank of bossy words. The learners have to select and write an appropriate one for each picture.

   **Answers:**
   a) kick    b) hop    c) jump/step    d) run

**Try this:** Refer the learners to the pictures on page 25 of the Learner's book. Explain that in each picture a child is saying a command sentence. Point out the three sentences in the box. The learners must decide which sentence to write in each speech bubble. Suggest that the learners work in pairs. They can talk about each picture and help each other decide.

### Success criteria ✓

While completing the activities, assess and record learners who can:

● engage in imaginative play, pretend to be a character in a shop and use appropriate words and gestures

● talk clearly to their partner.

## Further activities

● Repeat the shop situation but change the shop to one with computer games, mobile phones or outdoor play equipment. Remind the talk partners to both take a turn as shopkeeper and use command sentences.

● Supply new pictures representing these actions: skip, turn, roll, climb. Provide the words for the children to match correctly.

# Fiction or non-fiction?

Pages 26–27

Page 12

Learner's book

Workbook

## Objectives

- Show awareness that texts for different purposes look different, e.g. use of photographs, diagrams. (1Rv1)
- Identify separate sounds (phonemes) within words, which may be represented by more than one letter, e.g. 'th', 'ch', 'sh'. (1R03)
- Know the name and most common sounds associated with every letter in the English alphabet. (1R02)

## Starter

- Remind the learners of the word 'instructions'. Ask: *What do instructions do?* (They tell people to do things.) *What sort of words do they have?* (Bossy words.)

- Explain that an instruction can also tell you *how* to do something. Show the learners some sets of instructions. The instructions may be in a book of recipes, a book of science experiments, a 'how to make' book, or on display in your school (perhaps next to a fire extinguisher). Ask: *What is unusual about the way they are set out on a page?* (The writing is often set out as a list.) Choose some appropriate examples and ask: *What do you notice about the titles for these instructions?* (They use the word *how*.)

- Point out that instructions telling you how to do things still use bossy words. Read aloud some bossy words from your example sets of instructions. Include the bossy word 'show', emphasising the initial sound *sh*. Ask the learners to repeat just *sh*. Write the grapheme 'sh' for the learners to see. Explain that this is the written form of the phoneme (sound).

- Write the bossy words 'shut' and 'wash' on the board. Point to each grapheme as you sound out and blend the words, emphasising the *sh* sound. Point out that the letter group 'sh' begins one word and ends the other.

- Direct the learners to the Helpful hints box in the Learner's book on page 26. Read the box aloud as they follow. Point out 'How' in the titles, and the mention of photographs, lists and numbers. Ask: *Does this look different from a storybook?* (Yes.)

**Talk Partners**

**Look at a recipe book.** Put the learners into pairs. Make sure that each pair has a storybook and a short recipe book (or photocopy). Can they tell each other ways in which the books are different? Share their findings in a class discussion.

## Activity notes and answers

1. **Sound, blend and write instruction words.** Explain that the learners have to think of a bossy or instruction word to match the picture and write it. Suggest that partners help each other in thinking of the word. Saying the word to each other will remind them to sound out and blend the word before they write it.

   **Answers:**

   a) cut          b) push          c) pull          d) stick

# Reading and writing *th*

1. **Hear the unvoiced *th*.** Read the list of words aloud as the learners follow. Remind them of the image of the thumb in the Helpful hints box and practise the unvoiced *th* sound together. Read the list again, the learners following and repeating the words. Suggest working in pairs for the learners to read aloud to each other as they find and underline the sound in each word.

   **Answers:**
   thi<u>ng</u>
   pa<u>th</u>
   ma<u>ths</u>
   tee<u>th</u>
   clo<u>th</u>

2. **Complete the captions.**

   **Answers:**
   a) fish for lunch
   b) ship at sea
   c) toothbrush and cloth

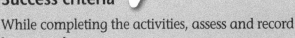

> **Success criteria** ✓
>
> While completing the activities, assess and record learners who can:
> - show they understand that instruction texts look different to story texts
> - identify words with the phoneme *th*.

**IT** Put the learners into small groups. Explain that the class is going to make a set of instructions telling other people how to find their classroom. With adult support, each group should use a digital camera or mobile phone to photograph some places on the route. Load all the pictures on to a computer for the learners to put into order.

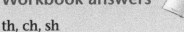
## Workbook answers

th, ch, sh

1.

| START | **shut** | sit | sells | sink | pink | pack | catch |
|-------|----------|------|--------|------|------|------|-------|
| miss | **shop** | **rush** | **posh** | hill | tree | put | bath |
| this | still | sing | **shall** | **she** | **shin** | had | chip |
| chin | bath | that | kick | stop | **mash** | sop | catch |
| pull | chip | then | tick | kind | **hush** | **rash** | think |
| cheese | tin | chill | pan | help | trust | **push** | **shell** |
| stick | till | stand | think | thing | watch | batch | **END** |

2. a) three    b) cherry    c) push

## Further activities

- Learners complete Workbook page 12.
- Give the learners a collection of words, only some of which use the *th* sound. Tell the learners how many they are looking for and to write them.
- Provide a 'how to' instruction text. Can the learners pick out four command words?
- Use your book corner or library. Put the learners in pairs and set the task of finding and copying the titles of two instruction books. Compare results. Do any titles begin with *How*?

# Reading instructions

Pages 28–31

Page 13

## Objectives

- Read a range of common words on sight. (1R10)
- Show awareness that texts for different purposes look different, e.g. use of photographs, diagrams. (1Rv1)

## Starter

- Remind the children what instruction texts are. (They tell you how to do something.)
- Direct the learners to pages 28 and 29 of the Learner's book, asking them to look only briefly at this instruction text. Ask: *What looks different from a storybook?* (Lists; types of pictures; numbers; layout of the text on the page.)
- Read pages 28 and 29 aloud as the learners follow. Discuss what the text does. (It tells you how to make chocolate fruit kebabs.) Point out the word *How* in the title. Explain that an instruction text often has a title beginning *How…*
- Read the text aloud again, encouraging the learners to join in when they can.
- Ask: *What is special about the words Peel, Put and Pour?* (They are all bossy words.) Ask the learners to write, without looking at the text again, the word *put*. Share ideas on ways they can remember how to spell it. (For example: saying sounds and blending them to build the word.) Let them use the blending process to write *peel*.
- Talk about the numbering of the sentences. Ask: *Do the sentences have to be in those places?* Encourage partner discussion and remind the learners to look at the Helpful hints box on page 26 of the Learner's book. Read the contents of the box together.

## Activity notes and answers

**Talk Partners**

**Read instructions and identify the right order.** Direct learners to the Talk Partners box on Learner's book page 30 and read aloud what they have to do. Reread pages 28–29, the learners joining in with you. Watch to see which sentences the learners point to as they do the tasks.

1. **Put sentences in order.** Let the learners read the sentences aloud, to themselves or a partner. Suggest they picture the actions in their minds to work out the order. After writing all three sentences, they need to read their whole text. Does the order make sense?

   **Answers:**

   b) Put on socks.     c) Put on shoes.     a) Go outside.

2. **Match the captions.** Remind the learners that a caption helps the reader to understand the picture.

   **Answers:**

   1 = c  Eat.

   2 = a  Cut up fruit.

   3 = b  Melt chocolate.

# Words

1. **Read and learn words.** Read the words in the cloud together. Encourage partners to exchange ideas on ways to learn how to spell the words. Blending, reading aloud, writing and checking will all help.

   **Answers:**
   a) with, when     b) the, this, there     c) with, this

2. **Fill in the gaps.** Explain that the learners can fill each gap with any word that makes sense. Reading the sentences aloud to themselves or a partner will help them to think of ideas. You may prompt further by reading the sentences aloud and the learners whispering a word to themselves or a partner. Some learners may need the help of a starting sound.

   **Possible answers:**
   a) Now put on a hat.
   b) Take this apple.
   c) Go up there.
   d) Sit with me.

## Success criteria

While completing the activities, assess and record learners who can:

- read a range of common words on sight
- show awareness that texts such as sets of instructions may look different from other texts.

## Workbook answers

**How to make crispy cakes**
1. Melt the chocolate.
2. Mix in the crispy rice.
3. Put in cases.
4. Leave to cool.
5. Eat.

## Further activities

- Learners complete Workbook page 13.
- Direct the learners to Learner's book page 29. Ask them to find the bossy word in each of the five lines of text.
- Play a game in which the learners are divided into teams, each team represented by a colour. In turn, ask teams to write one of the words from the cloud on Learner's book page 31. A correct answer wins a team star; an incorrect answer gives another team a go. Keep the game light-hearted and be ready to promote success by repeating words you have already used.
- Provide a bank of ten common words. Write five short sentences on the board, a word missing in each. Ask the learners to choose from the bank and write the complete sentences.
- Write, in a numbered list, a set of *How to make …* instructions, but in the wrong order. The learners must list and number them correctly.

## Assessment idea

Create a worksheet called Building Words. Write three graphemes, but leave the graphemes separate as if in their own houses. For example:

 *cut*

Explain to the learners that they push a line of houses together, and then say and write the words they have made.

| Houses | | | Answers: |
|---|---|---|---|
| p | u | ll | pull |
| wh | e | n | when |
| th | i | s | this |
| b | i | g | big |
| y | e | s | yes |
| c | u | t | cut |

# Using *and*

 Pages 32–33

 Pages 14–15

## Objectives

- Write sentence-like structures which may be joined by *and*. (1Wp3)
- Form letters correctly. (1W02)

## Starter

- Hold up a page of writing. Point out that the writing consists of words divided into groups. Ask: *What are these groups?* (Sentences.)
- Explain that a sentence is a group of words that makes sense because it sounds complete. Give the learners an example. Write these on the board:

  some fruit kebabs

  We made some fruit kebabs.

  Ask: *Which one makes sense and sounds complete?* (The second one.)
- Display a paragraph of text divided into three sentences. Ask the learners to tell partners how many sentences there are. Agree on the answer. Ask: *How can you check quickly?* (You count the full stops.)
- Explain that a sentence begins with a capital letter and ends with a full stop. Point to examples in the text on display.

## Activity notes and answers

**Helpful hints:** Direct the learners to the Helpful hints box on page 32 of the Learner's book. Read the hint together. Make up a sentence that tells the learners to do two things. For example: *Look at me and listen.* Say it again. Did the learners notice *and*?

1. **Find 'and' in the text.** With the learners, read aloud the task. Some learners may prefer to do the search with a partner. Suggest they write down the correct line and underline *and*.

   **Answer:** Peel the fruit <u>and</u> cut it up.

2. **Find 'and' in sentences.** Suggest that partners read the sentence together, write it and look for and underline *and*.

   **Answers:**
   a) Get off the bus <u>and</u> go to the shop.
   b) Take the coat <u>and</u> bag from the peg.
   c) See the duck <u>and</u> frog on the pond.
   d) Please get the bat <u>and</u> ball.

3. **Use 'and' to add to sentences.** Explain that the sentence endings are in the clouds. Can the learners sort out which goes where? Suggest that reading aloud quietly to themselves or a partner will help them decide. Ask: *What will you put at the end of each sentence?* (A full stop.)

   Read all the text aloud for the learners to follow before they start.

   **Answers:**
   a) Find the pens and paper.
   b) Wash your hands and eat your fruit.
   c) Feed the sheep and goats.
   d) Sit on the rug and listen.

# Writing words and sentences

1. **Join sentences with 'and'.** Direct the learners to activity 1 on Learner's book page 33. Read the instructions in a) aloud. Ask: *How many sentences are there at first?* (Two.) *How many when they are joined?* (One.) *What is the joining word?* (and) *What happens to some words?* (They are left out of the new joined sentence.) *How many full stops are there now?* (One.) Let the learners work in pairs to help each other complete the activity.

   **Answers:**
   a) Take your bag and hat.
   b) I like apples and bananas.
   c) The ball is big and red.
   d) Shut the door and sit down.

**Writing presentation:** Stand with your back to the learners, your finger forming the letters 't' and 'h' in the air. Ask the learners to copy by writing in the air. If another adult is available to model letter formation, move among the learners, checking and adjusting their movements.

## Success criteria

While completing the activities, assess and record learners who can:

* write sentences containing *and* and a full stop
* write the words with correct letter formation.

## Workbook answers

**Longer sentences**

b) I have a big brother and a little sister.

   or

   I have a big brother and I have a little sister.
c) Eat your beans and drink your milk.
d) Read the book and tell me about it.
e) Pick up the cup and give it to me.

## Further activities

* Learners complete Workbook pages 14–15.
* Write a list of sentences using *and*. Ask the learners to circle *and*.
* Write a list of pairs of sentences that the learners must join with *and*. When they read the new sentence aloud, should any words be left out? Do they know how many full stops to use?
* Do activity 3 on Learner's book page 32 again. This time, invite the learners to finish the sentences with their own words.

## Assessment ideas

Ask the learners to put these sentences together with *and*.

1. Take your pen. Take your pencil.
2. I have books. I have paper.
3. The school is big. The school is hot.
4. Open the book. Read the words.
5. My cat is black. My cat is small.
6. Get some flowers. Get some chocolates.

**Answers:**

1. Take your pen and pencil.
2. I have books and paper.
3. The school is big and hot.
4. Open the book and read the words.
5. My cat is black and small.
6. Get some flowers and chocolates.

# Reading non-fiction

 Pages 34–36

Learner's book

## Objectives

- Use phonic knowledge to read decodable words and to attempt to sound out some elements of unfamiliar words. (1R06)
- Listen carefully to questions and instructions. (1SL8)
- Read labels, lists and captions to find information. (1Rx1)

## Starter

- Point out the subheading at the top of page 34 of the Learner's book: 'Reading non-fiction'. Explain that fiction means stories. Can they work out what non-fiction must be? (Writing that is not a story, but is about something that is true.)

- Direct the learners to the title of the non-fiction text on page 34 of the Learner's book. Read it aloud to the learners. Ask: *What sort of non-fiction text is this going to be? How did you guess?* (An instruction text because *How* is at the start of the title.)

- Put the learners into pairs to look at the rest of the text. Encourage them just to look, not read. Ask partners to tell each other what other clues they can see that tell them this is an instruction text. Share ideas as a class, mentioning: the list layout; numbers; pictures.

- Draw attention to the first three words of the text. Can the learners read them? Explain that this heading is another clue that this is an instruction text; a 'how to' instruction text usually has this heading at the beginning. Ask: *What do you expect underneath the heading?* (A list of what the reader needs.)

- Return to the title of the text. Can the learners tell a partner what a forward roll is? Invite explanations and ask the learners if any of them have ever done a forward roll. Did they need adult help?

- Read the instruction text aloud as the learners follow. Read it again, giving time for the learners to check the picture with each line of writing. Ask: *Do you find these instructions clear? Do you think you know how to do a forward roll now? What has helped you?* Give partners time to share views before you accept answers from the class. Make it clear that the pictures support the words.

# Giving instructions

## Activity notes and answers

1. **Find bossy words.** Put the learners into pairs and focus their attention on the instruction text on Learner's book pages 34–35. Explain that you are going to say what they have to look for; they must then point to the correct place in the text. Read each line from activity 1 on page 36, watching to see where the learners point. Progress to the learners listening to you and showing each other that they know where these words and pictures are. Finish with one partner reading activity 1 with you, the other pointing and showing.

   **Answers:**
   a) <u>Stand up</u> in a large flat area.
      <u>Bend</u> your knees.
      <u>Bend</u> your elbows.
      Quickly <u>push</u> off and <u>roll</u> over onto your back and then to your feet.

b) A large flat area, sports clothes.

c) Drop your head and tuck in your chin.

d) The picture with line 5.

2. **Choose words to complete sentences.** Read the instruction aloud as the learners follow. Suggest that partners read their answers to each other. The listener will be able to say if the speaker has given an instruction.

**Answers:**

a) Stand up.

b) Roll over quickly.

c) Bend your legs.

**Make up an exercise pattern.** Read this section on Learner's book page 36 aloud as the learners follow. Ask them to think about their movement and P.E. lessons. What actions do they do? Ask them to work out a short routine of jumps, skips and hops. Put the learners into pairs, one as teacher and one as the learner. The 'teacher' must give oral instructions for jumps, skips and hops. Does the 'learner' follow correctly? Let the learners swap roles.

**Success criteria** ✓

While completing the activities, assess and record learners who can:

● use phonic knowledge to help them read the instruction text

● listen carefully to follow their partner's instructions.

## Further activities

● Extend the *Talk Partners* activity on Learner's book 36 as partners prepare a set of instructions for the class to follow in P.E. Provide a bank of command words. Invite the learners to use one at the start of each line.

● Set learners the challenge of reading some parts of the instruction text on Learner's book pages 34–35 independently. Encourage them to use their phonic knowledge to sound out unfamiliar words.

● Follow up the *Talk Partners* activity on Learner's book page 36 by asking speakers to assess how well their instructions are listened to and followed by their partners.

## Assessment ideas

Observe the learners doing the *Talk Partners* work. Assess their ability to give, listen to and follow instructions.

# Two letters – one sound

Learner's book
Page 37

## Objectives

- Identify separate sounds (phonemes) within words, which may be represented by more than one letter, e.g. 'th', 'ch', 'sh'. (1R03)

## Starter

- Ask the learners if they remember what a phoneme is? Explain that a phoneme is another name for a sound.

- Explain that some phonemes are made by just one letter; other phonemes are made by two letters written side-by-side and working together to make the sound.

- Put your finger to your lips. Ask: *What phoneme am I making? (sh)* Let the learners practise making this sound. Do they know which two letters are written for the phoneme? ('sh'). Can partners tell each other a word beginning with the *sh* phoneme. Share results and write some on the board. For example: shut, shop, ship.

- Make the sound *ch* for the learners to copy. Ask: *Which two letters do you write for this phoneme?* ('ch'). Ask partners to tell each other a word beginning with the *ch* phoneme. Share results and write some on the board. For example: chin, chop, chick.

- Do the same for the unvoiced *th* phoneme. Make the sound for the learners to repeat. Ask: *Which two letters do you write for this phoneme?* ('th'). Write some examples on the board: thumb, thin, thick.

- In turn, talk about four other sounds that are sometimes made by two letters: *l, s, k, f.* Say the *s* sound aloud for the learners to repeat. Ask them to listen for the sound when you say a word: kiss. Can they tell a partner if the *s* sound came at the beginning or end of the word? (End.) Write the word on the board and read it together. *How many written letters make the s phoneme in this word?* (Two, 'ss'.)

- Do this for the sound *k.* Let the learners practise saying it before you say the word *pick* for them to hear the sound at the end of the word. Write the word on the board and read it together. *How many letters make the k phoneme in this word?* (Two, 'ck'.)

- Model the *l* phoneme for the learners to repeat. Ask them to identify the sound when you say the word *fill.* Write the word on the board and read it together. Ask: *Which two written letters make the sound?* ('ll'.)

- Practise the sound *f* together. Say *cuff* for the learners to hear the phoneme's place in the word. (The end.) Write the word on the board and read it together. *How many letters make the f phoneme in this written word?* (Two, 'ff'.)

## Activity notes and answers

**Helpful hints:** Direct the learners to the Helpful hints box on page 37 of the Learner's book. Explain that the graphemes (written letter groups) are in bold on the left – words containing them are in bold on the right. Emphasise that each grapheme on the right stands for one sound (phoneme). Say the sound and the word at the end of the line as the children follow. Ask: *Can you hear the sound at the end or at the start of the word?*

1. **Match letters to phonemes.** Explain that the learners will be looking for pairs of letters that make one sound. Read aloud the words. Ask the learners to write the words. Read them aloud again for the learners to repeat. Which sound can they hear that is made by two letters? Suggest that working with a partner will help.

   **Answers:**

   sa<u>ck</u>   pu<u>ff</u>   <u>ch</u>um   o<u>ff</u>   le<u>ss</u>   be<u>ll</u>   do<u>ll</u>   ro<u>ck</u>et   du<u>ll</u>
   se<u>ll</u>   me<u>ss</u>   fu<u>ss</u>   <u>sh</u>o<u>ck</u>

2. **Finish words.** Read aloud the instructions. Write the pairs of letters on the board and say the sounds together. Suggest working with a partner and saying words aloud as they choose letters for the spaces. Be ready to offer adult support when needed. Check that the learners can read their finished words.

   **Answers:**

   a) hi<u>ss</u>                e) <u>sh</u>eep

   b) hi<u>ll</u>                f) mo<u>th</u>

   c) cli<u>ff</u>               g) <u>ch</u>illy

   d) ki<u>ck</u>

---

**Success criteria** ✓

While completing the activities, assess and record learners who can:

- identify the phonemes made from two letters in the words.

---

## Further activities

- Put the learners into pairs. Direct them to the Helpful hints box on page 37 of the Learner's book. Ask them to read the words in bold to each other before drawing a picture for each. Encourage them to blend sounds to build the whole word.

- Give the learners a new list of words that have two letters making one phoneme. Ask them to underline the letters making the phoneme:

  trick, fuss, tell, dish, well, bucket, dress, sheet, teeth

  **Answers:**

  tri<u>ck</u>, fu<u>ss</u>, te<u>ll</u>, di<u>sh</u>, we<u>ll</u>, bu<u>ck</u>et, dre<u>ss</u>, <u>sh</u>eet, tee<u>th</u>

# How to make a butterfly

Pages 38–39

Pages 16–17

**Objectives**

- Write for a purpose using some basic features of text type. (1Wa5)
- Write simple information texts with labels, captions, lists, questions and instructions for a purpose. (1Wa6)

## Starter

- Draw attention to the title on page 38 of the Learner's book: *How to make a butterfly*. Point out the starting word 'How'. Ask: *What type of text do you expect?* (An instruction text.) Remind the learners that 'How to' instructions often have a title beginning with 'How'.

- Invite the learners to look quickly at the instructions on page 38. Ask: *What is surprising?* (There are no words.) What would you expect? (Sentences as well as these pictures.)

- Look together at the pictures and question the learners about them. Ask about the items in picture 1. *Why are they shown first?* (They are what the reader needs.) Point to the final picture, showing a pattern being painted. Ask: *How does the last picture help you paint a pattern?* (It shows that the butterfly's wings must match.)

- Talk about the order of the pictures. Why is the picture of a spoon, paper, paint, pipe cleaners and glue first? (The reader has to know what to have.) Why is picture 3 before picture 4? (You have to cut out wings before you can stick them on.) Agree that the pictures are shown in the order that the reader must do those things.

- Ask the learners if they remember what sort of things to include in an instruction text. Prompt them by directing them to pages 28–29 of the Learner's book. Discuss its layout; lists; command words; numbers; helpful pictures; a 'You will need' section; a 'What to do' heading. Identify examples of these things in the instruction text on pages 28–29 of the Learner's book.

## Activity notes and answers

**Talk about making a wooden spoon butterfly.** Put the learners into pairs to discuss page 38 of the Learner's book. Do they think these instructions are good? Could they follow them? How would they improve them? Invite partners to present their ideas to another pair of learners or to the whole class.

1. **Follow instructions.** Make sure that you have all the materials and set aside an extended period of time. It will be easier to manage if the learners work in pairs. After making their butterflies, ask the learners to produce the instruction text in stages:
   - A title and a picture of the finished item.
   - A 'You will need' heading and a list of those things.
   - The 'What to do' heading.
   - Numbered pictures of the stages of making their butterfly spoon.
   - Finally, let the learners work out the wording for their caption sentences. Remind them to use the words given to help them and to use 'and' as a joining word. Emphasise that each caption sentence needs a command word.

**What have I learnt?** Read the checklist on Learner's book page 39 aloud for the learners to follow. Then encourage partners to read it together as they check their instruction texts and assess how complete they are. You may suggest they put a tick or a score out of five if they have included something.

## Success criteria ✓

While completing the activities, assess and record learners who can:

- write a set of instructions in an ordered list and with command words using some basic features of text type
- write captions for the pictures with a set of instructions.

## Workbook answers

**How to make a bead necklace**

You will need: two beads of each colour

3.  Thread two red beads onto the string.
4.  Thread two green beads onto the string.
5.  Thread two blue beads onto the string.

## Further activities

- Learners complete Workbook page 16.
- Put the learners in pairs. Ask them to discuss the instructions they have written and drawn, and compare them with those on page 38 of the Learner's book. Which instructions would they prefer to use? Why?
- Ask the learners to look at their results from *What I have learnt?* Can they identify what they did well last time? How could they do better when they create another instruction text?
- Let the learners think of a new item that could be made with a wooden spoon, paper, paint and glue. They must write the instructions. Suggest that they do the work in the same order as activity 1 on page 39 of the Learner's book.
- Learners complete the Self-assessment table on page 17 of the Workbook.

# Unit 3 Simple rhymes

## Objectives Overview

| Learning Objective | Objective Code | Learner's book Activities | Teacher's pack Activities | Workbook Activities |
|---|---|---|---|---|
| **Reading** | | | | |
| Identify separate sounds (phonemes) within words, which may be represented by more than one letter, e.g. 'th', 'ch', 'sh'. | 1R03 | 42 | 47 | 19 |
| Use knowledge of sounds to read and write single syllable words with short vowels. | 1R04 | 42 | 47 | 19 |
| Demonstrate an understanding that one spoken word corresponds with one written word. | 1R07 | 40, 48 | 47, 54 | |
| Join in with reading familiar, simple stories and poems. | 1R08 | 40, 48 | 47, 50, 54 | |
| Read a range of common words on sight. | 1R10 | 40 | 47 | 20 |
| Learn and recite simple poems. | 1R14 | 41, 44, 49 | 47, 50, 54 | 18 |
| Join in and extend rhymes and refrains, playing with language patterns. | 1R15 | 47, 49 | 52 | 21 |
| Talk about significant aspects of a story's language, e.g. repetitive refrain, rhyme, patterned language. | 1Rw1 | 46, 48 | 52, 54 | |
| **Writing** | | | | |
| Develop a comfortable and efficient pencil grip. | 1W01 | 43 | 47 | |
| Know that a capital letter is used for *I*, for proper nouns and for the start of a sentence. | 1W03 | 49 | 54 | 22 |
| Use knowledge of sounds to write simple regular words, and to attempt other words including when writing simple sentences dictated by the teacher from memory. | 1W04 | 42 | 47 | |
| Use relevant vocabulary. | 1Wa2 | 49 | 54 | |
| Compose and write a simple sentence with a capital letter and a full stop. | 1Wp2 | 49 | 55 | |
| Use rhyme and relate this to spelling patterns. | 1Ws3 | 41, 43, 46 | 47, 48, 52 | |
| **Speaking and listening** | | | | |
| Show some awareness of the listener through non-verbal communication. | 1SL3 | | | 18 |
| Answer questions and explain further when asked. | 1SL4 | 45 | 50 | |
| Take turns in speaking. | 1SL6 | 45 | 51 | |

# Round and round the mango tree

Pages 40–43

Pages 18–20

## Objectives

- Demonstrate an understanding that one spoken word corresponds with one written word. (1R07)
- Join in with reading familiar, simple stories and poems. (1R08)
- Read a range of common words on sight. (1R10)
- Learn and recite simple poems. (1R14)
- Identify separate sounds (phonemes) within words, which may be represented by more than one letter, e.g. 'th', 'ch', 'sh'. (1R03)
- Use knowledge of sounds to read and write single syllable words with short vowels. (1R04)
- Use knowledge of sounds to write simple regular words, and to attempt other words including when writing simple sentences dictated by the teacher from memory. (1W04)
- Develop a comfortable and efficient pencil grip. (1W01)

## Starter

- Ask the learners if they know what a nursery rhyme is. Explain that it is a simple poem often read or said to young children as the words are easy to remember. Ask: *Do you know any nursery rhymes?* Let partners exchange answers before you share information as a class.

- Use the word 'rhyme' again. Ask: *What is special about words that rhyme?* (They end in the same sound.) Give examples, gradually pausing for longer to say a second word so that the learners can provide one before you do: *'bed' and 'head'; 'gate' and 'wait'; 'win' and ... 'bin'; 'cat' and ... 'hat'.*

- Write h**a**t on the board. Ask: *What sound does the letter in bold make.* Agree on *a.* Write these words on the board, the vowel always in bold: r**e**d, h**o**t, c**u**t, b**i**g. Invite the learners to make the sound of each letter in bold.

- Put the learners into pairs with five large cards. Each card should have one of the written graphemes: 'a', 'e', 'i', 'o', 'u'. Play a game in which you say one of these short vowel sounds: partners decide which of their cards has the written form, and hold it up.

- Direct the learners to page 40 of the Learner's book. Read the title and the poem aloud as the learners follow. Who knows this nursery rhyme? Read it aloud again, the learners following the lines with a finger below each word as you reach it. Reread it, the learners still using a finger to keep in time with the words, but also joining in with the reading as much as they can. Emphasise that even if they know this nursery rhyme by heart, you still want them to have a finger under each word as they get to it.

## Activity notes and answers

**Read and learn the rhyme.** Direct the learners to the *Talk Partners* box on page 41 of the Learner's book. Suggest partners help each other with reading and listening to each other. One partner may read one line; the other may say the next one from memory.

1. **Match numbers and words.** Suggest partners read the words to each other before they match them to numbers. Offer adult support only if needed.

   **Answers:** five – 5, one – 1, four – 4, three – 3, two – 2

2. **Find words that rhyme.** Can the learners tell a partner what 'rhyme' means? Confirm that rhyming words end in the same sound. Point out the cloud and explain that the words are all from the poem on page 40. Ask partners to work together to identify the rhyming pairs.

   **Answers:**
   tail – pail
   me – tree

# Write short words

1. **Change phonemes.** Put the learners in pairs to read the words in the cloud. Explain that they must now change a phoneme (sound) in the word to a new phoneme and make a new word. Read the phoneme instructions one at a time so that partners help each other. Accept oral answers before progressing to writing.

   **Answers:**
   a) ten
   b) dip
   c) leg
   d) his
   e) than

2. **Write words.** Agree on the content of the pictures. Provide a collection of words written on the board, their middle letters missing. The learners must find and write the correct word, adding the missing letters.

   **Answers:**

   fish, ten, cat, duck, back

# Holding a pencil

1. **Read words.** Point out the list of words in the cloud. Read the questions to be answered with the words. Some learners may need partner support.

   **Answers:**
   a) who        b) who        c) my

**Writing presentation:** Remind the learners to grip their pencil comfortably so that they form letters correctly. Point out the picture in the Helpful hints box.

**Success criteria** ✔

While completing the activities, assess and record learners who can:
- join in with reading the poem
- use knowledge of sounds to read and write simple regular words
- read some common words on sight and attempt other words
- hold a pencil correctly when writing.

## Workbook answers

### Five little peas

2. pressed – rest
   stop – POP!

### Reading blends

1. a) drip
   b) chimp
   c) frog
   d) clap

2. a) pond
   b) chest

### Common words search

| u | k | n | o | n | e | n | e |
|---|---|---|---|---|---|---|---|
| s | o | s | n | u | s | a | w |
| k | e | j | e | i | e | l | n |
| s | g | o | o | y | o | u | r |
| o | q | n | l | w | p | o | k |
| l | i | t | t | l | e | k | e |
| g | u | g | e | m | o | l | d |
| d | t | h | e | n | k | d | x |
| q | f | j | a | d | j | m | y |
| r | t | t | h | a | t | w | l |
| x | h | m | l | j | u | s | t |

**IT** Play nursery rhymes on *www.bbc.co.uk/schoolradio/subjects/earlylearning/nurserysongs*. This will allow you to check that the learners are pointing to the correct words.

## Further activities

- Learners complete Workbook pages 18–20.
- Move on from activity 1 on Learner's book page 41 by matching digits 6–10 to their words.
- Put the learners into groups to practise saying the nursery rhyme by heart and to rehearse a performance.
- Hold a poetry recital, each group performing for the class. Groups may include movements in their performance.
- Read other nursery rhymes with the learners (see Book list below).

### Book list

- *Usborne Illustrated Book of Nursery Rhymes* by Felicity Brooks (Usborne Publishing Ltd)
- *Off to the Sweet Shores of Africa* by Uzo Unobagha (Chronicle Books)

# Row, row, row your boat

Pages 44–45

## Objectives

- Learn and recite simple poems. (1R14)
- Answer questions and explain further when asked. (1SL4)

## Starter

- Explain that nursery rhymes and other simple poems are intended to be read to and by children. Therefore the subjects and words are not usually very serious.

- Point out that some of these poems were written a long time ago. People have learnt them by heart and spoken them, but may have changed some lines or added new words of their own. That is why there are sometimes many versions of the same poem.

- Many of the poems have been written with the expectation that the reader will join in, not just with the words but perhaps some actions.

- Direct the learners to page 40 of the Learner's book and read or recite the poem together. Ask: *What action could you do?* Let partners exchange ideas before having a class discussion. Invite learners to demonstrate: perhaps running on the spot and jumping like a monkey.

- Read 'Round and round the mango tree' again, the learners joining in with their chosen action.

- Remind the learners of how they recited this poem to a partner or in a group. Ask: *How did you try to speak?* (Clearly)

- Put the learners into pairs to hold one–two minute conversations. They must each ask and answer a question about the things they like to do or the places they like going to in the school holidays.

- Afterwards discuss the conversations. Ask: *Did your partner ask a clear question that you could answer? Did they look interested in your answer? How did they show they were paying attention?* Make sure that clear speech, eye contact and concentration are all mentioned.

- Direct the learners to page 44 of the Learner's book. Read the title and the poem aloud as the learners follow. (Leave out the words in brackets.) Ask: *Who knows this nursery rhyme?* Point out and read the words in brackets. Suggest that they are a way for the reader to be part of the poem. Read the poem together, this time making the noises.

## Activity notes and answers

1. **Learn the poem by heart.** Read 'Row, row, row your boat' together. Put the learners into pairs to practise saying some lines without looking at the text at first, then all of it.

# Answering questions

1. **Answer questions.** Read the questions aloud, for the partners to each give each other answers. They may look back at the poem if they want to. As they answer each other, move among the pairs, prompting, supporting and reminding about clear speech. Allow enough time between a and d.

   **Answers:**
   a) In a boat. The boat is going down the stream.
   b) Yes. The word *merrily*.
   c) Crocodile. No.
   d) Roar.

**Discuss a poem.** Direct the learners to the *Talk Partners* box on page 45 of the Learner's book. Suggest that they each have a turn asking and answering the questions. Emphasise that careful listening is important. For e), they could each ask two new questions. Be ready to suggest starting words.

## Success criteria ✔

While completing the activities, assess and record learners who can:

- learn and recite the poem
- answer questions about the poem and think of their own questions.

Play nursery rhymes on *www.bbc.co.uk/schoolradio/subjects/earlylearning/nurserysongs*. Is this version exactly the same? Compare another online version of the poem.

## Further activities

- Return to the *Talk Partners* box on Learner's book page 45. Ask partners to repeat the activity, but this time to record the answers they are given with simple words or pictures.
- Check the illustration on page 44 of the Learner's book. Ask the learners to create their own.
- Put the learners into pairs to act out the poem as you read it aloud. Invite some pairs to perform for the class. What questions do the class want to ask them?
- The book listed in the Book list below provides a sing-along version of the rhyme for the learners to follow.

## Assessment ideas

Put the learners into small groups so that you can observe and listen to individuals. Read the poem together. Ask each learner three questions, assessing their understanding and ability to answer. Questions could include: *What should the person in the poem do if they see a crocodile? Where will the crocodile be? Where will the lion be? What would you take with you to eat? Would you need a friend? Why?*

## Book list

- *Row, row, row your boat* by David Ellwand (Silver Dolphin)

# Patterns in poems

**Learner's book** Pages 46–47

**Workbook** Page 21

## Objectives

- Talk about significant aspects of a story's language, e.g. repetitive refrain, rhyme, patterned language. (1Rw1)
- Join in and extend rhymes and refrains, playing with language patterns. (1R15)
- Use rhyme and relate this to spelling patterns. (1Ws3)

## Starter

- Explain that most simple poems and nursery rhymes have some patterns in them. Ask: *What does 'pattern' mean?* Let partners share ideas before you invite answers from the class. Define pattern as something that appears again and again; a pattern repeats.
- Suggest that patterns or repetition make a poem easier to learn by heart. Can the learners think why? (After saying a line or word once, it is easier to remember the next time.)
- Direct the learners to 'Round and round the mango tree' on page 40 of the Learner's book. Read or recite the poem together. Ask: *Do you know most of this poem by heart now?* In the poem, point to examples of rhyming couplets (pairs of lines) that make it easy to remember.
- Explain that in some poems, words are repeated.
- Recite together the poem *Row, row, row your boat* on page 44 of the Learner's book. Ask: *Can you hear one another using lots of repetition?* (Yes) Leave detailed investigation of the patterns for the learners to do independently in the activities.

## Activity notes and answers

1. **Count and use repetition.** Explain to the learners that they are working from activity 1 on page 46 of the Learner's book, but they will need to keep looking back at page 44. Suggest that they do their counting, write an answer, then count again. Partner work may be helpful.

   **Answers:**
   a) three
   b) two
   c) four
   d) two

2. **Pair rhymes.** Ask: *What is special about words that rhyme?* (They end in the same sound.) Explain that the words do not have to look the same; it is how they sound that matters. Therefore saying the words aloud, to themselves or a partner, is important. Read aloud, as the learners follow, the list of words. Suggest using the pictures on page 47 of the Learner's book to give them answer clues as they write the pairs.

   **Answers:**
   beach, screech
   river, shiver
   creek, squeak

# My rhyme

1. **Complete the verses.** Remind the learners of their pairs of rhymes in activity 2 on Learner's book page 46. Explain that they will use them in the poem opposite. Read each verse aloud for partners to decide what to write. The pictures will help them.

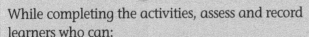

### Success criteria

While completing the activities, assess and record learners who can:

- identify the rhyming words
- complete new rhyming verses for the poem.

**Answers:**

Row, row, row your boat
Gently to the **beach.**
If you see a shark there
Don't forget to **screech.**

Row, row, row your boat
Gently down the **river.**
If you see a polar bear
Don't forget to **shiver.**

Row, row, row your boat
Gently down the **creek.**
If you see a little mouse
Don't forget to **squeak.**

### Further activities

- Learners complete Workbook page 21.
- Ask the learners to count how many times they can see these words in the poem: Don't forget.
- Read these words aloud and write them on the board in a random order for the learners to put into rhyming pairs and illustrate: puddle, lake, pool, muddle, shake, cool.

### Workbook answers

**Sunshine on the green grass**

1. <u>Sunshine on the</u> green grass.
   <u>Sunshine on the</u> tree.
   <u>Sunshine on the</u> rooftop –
   But NOT on me!

### Assessment ideas

Give the learners a worksheet with the following rhyme. They must complete the lines of the poem with rhyming words. Can they add a new verse of their own?

**Buzz, buzz, buzz**

Buzz, buzz, buzz,
Who's flying at me?
Buzz, buzz, buzz.
It must be a _____ .

Hiss, hiss, hiss,
In grass by the lake.
Hiss, hiss, hiss,
It must be a _____ .

Squeak, squeak, squeak,
From inside the house.
Squeak, squeak, squeak,
It must be a _____ .

Croak, croak, croak,
On the river log.
Croak, croak, croak,
It must be a _____ .

**Suggested answers** (but accept any words that rhyme)
bee, mouse, snake, frog

# I am the music man

Pages 48–51

Pages 22–23

## Objectives

- Use relevant with language patterns. (1Wa2)
- Know that a capital letter is used for *I*, for proprer nouns and for the start of a sentence. (1W03)
- Demonstrate an understanding that one spoken word corresponds with one written word. (1R07)
- Join in with reading familiar, simple stories and poems. (1R08)
- Learn and recite simple poems. (1R14)
- Talk about significant aspects of a story's language, e.g. repetitive refrain, rhyme, patterned language. (1Rw1)

## Starter

- Write some pairs of upper and lower case letters on the board, or show the learners an alphabet poster with the upper and lower case of each letter. Make it clear that both the upper case letters and their equivalent lower case letters make the same sound.

- Point to pairs of letters. For each pair, ask: *Which form of the letter do you usually write?* (Lower case) Explain when to use the upper case: to start a sentence and for special words such as names.

- Write this on the board: *In the morning, Kym set off for the market. She needed some beans and red peppers.* Ask the learners to count upper case letters and to hold up an answer on their fingers. Underline the three upper case forms, and ask the learners to tell you why it was used each time.

- Direct the learners to page 40 of the Learner's book. Point out the capital letters to start each line; explain that this is usual in poetry. Ask: *Who know this poem by heart now? What pattern made it easy to learn?* (Pairs of rhyming lines.) Move to page 44 and ask the same questions about *Row, row row your boat*. Suggest that repetition is very helpful in this poem. Ask: *Which line is used in every verse?* (The first line.) *Which line is very similar in each verse?* (Its second.)

- Explain that even when words are not repeated they are still chosen carefully, for what they mean or the way they sound. Direct the learners to page 48 of the Learner's book and read the poem aloud as the learners follow. Ask: *Why do you think some of these words are used?* (For the way they sound.) *What repetition can you see?* (The line *I am the music man*; the words *I can play*.)

## Activity notes and answers

1. **Find repetition.** Read *I am the music man* again, the learners following with a finger and then joining in. Emphasise the need to check the poem more than once. They may prefer to work in pairs.

   **Answer:**
   *I am the music man*
   *I come from down your way*
   *And I can play...*
   *What can you play?*

2. **Enjoy a poem.** Put the learners into small groups.

   a) Suggest they begin by reading aloud the poem, helping one another say and gradually get to know the words. Point out that the repetition will make it easier to learn by heart.

   b) Talk as a class about musical instruments. Show pictures of a trombone, triangle and violin. Ask: *Who knows how to play them?* Let group members practise making the instruments' noises.

   c) Ask groups to imagine playing the three instruments and to practise the movements.

3. **Use capital letters.** Remind the learners of the rules for using capital letters and point out the Helpful hints box.

   **Answers:**
   a) May I come?
   b) I will go.
   c) Here I am?

**Success criteria**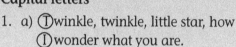

While completing the activities, assess and record learners who can use:

- relevant vocabulary
- capital letters appropriately.

**Further activities**

- Learners complete Workbook page 22.
- Ask the learners to share tips with a partner for learning poems by heart. Can they write and illustrate three helpful tips?
- Choose a different instrument to play in this poem. What action is needed? What noise will it make? What will the sound be in writing? Ask the learners to write a new verse.
- Put the learners into groups to rehearse a performance of *I am the music man* with actions and instrument noises. Let each group perform for the rest of the class.

**Workbook answers**

**Capital letters**

1. a) Twinkle, twinkle, little star, how I wonder what you are.

   b) Jack and Jill went up the hill.

   c) Little Bo-Peep has lost her sheep.

   d) Humpty-Dumpty sat on a wall.

2. I like my porridge hot.

   I like a milkshake cold.

   I like my sister Caroline,

   Although she's rather old.

   (The last line can begin with or without a capital letter.)

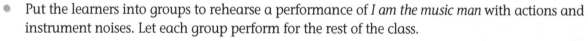

**Assessment ideas**

- Learners complete the Self-assessment table on page 23 of the Workbook.
- Learners complete Quiz 1 on pages 50–51 of the Learner's book. The answers follow on the next page.

# Quiz 1

## Answers:

1. a) We sat on the sand. We had an ice cream. **Middle**
   b) We went home. **End**
   c) Mum and I went to the seaside. **Beginning**

2. a) wish
   b) teeth
   c) chop
   d) wash
   e) path

3. a) The girl has a can of pop.
   b) The pot is hot.
   c) I will get to the top.
   d) Jon and I hop to the shop.

4. a) The fox is big and red.
   b) I have a fish and a shell in my net.
   c) I like to hop and jump.
   d) The boy has a book and pen.

5. **Example answers:**
   a) The man ran in the sun.
   b) The cat sat on the mat.
   c) The car was in a traffic jam.
   d) The map is on my lap.

6. net, vet
   pot, not
   shop, hop
   fell, shell

# Unit 4 Traditional stories

## Objectives Overview

| Learning Objective | Objective Code | Learner's book Activities | Teacher's pack Activities | Workbook Activities |
|---|---|---|---|---|
| **Reading** | | | | |
| Blend to read, and segment to spell, words with final and initial adjacent consonants, e.g. *b-l, n-d*. | 1R05 | 54, 67 | 58, 69 | 25 |
| Use phonic knowledge to read decodable words and to attempt to sound out some elements of unfamiliar words. | 1R06 | 58, 59 | | |
| Demonstrate an understanding that one spoken word corresponds with one written word. | 1R07 | 52, 53, 58, 59 | 58 | 28 |
| Join in with reading familiar, simple stories and poems. | 1R08 | 52, 53, 58, 59 | 58, 59, 62 | 28 |
| Read a range of common words on sight. | 1R10 | 54, 55 | 58, 60 | 26 |
| Retell stories, with some appropriate use of story language. | 1R13 | 61, 63 | 65, 67 | 30 |
| Pause at full stops when reading. | 1R17 | 64, 65 | 67 | |
| Anticipate what happens next in a story. | 1Ri1 | 52 | 58 | 24 |
| Talk about events in a story and make simple inferences about characters and events to show understanding. | 1Ri2 | 60, 65 | 60, 62, 63, 67 | |
| Talk about significant aspects of a story's language, e.g. repetitive refrain, rhyme, patterned language. | 1Rw1 | 61, 63 | 64, 65 | 29 |
| Recognise story elements, e.g. beginning, middle and end. | 1Rw2 | 60, 62, 63 | 62, 65 | 28, 29 |
| **Writing** | | | | |
| Form letters correctly. | 1W02 | 67 | 69 | 25 |
| Write simple storybooks with sentences to caption pictures. | 1Wa1 | 69 | 71 | |
| Begin to use some formulaic language, e.g. *Once upon a time.* | 1Wa4 | 63 | 65 | |
| Write a sequence of sentences retelling a familiar story or recounting an experience. | 1Wt1 | 57 | 60 | |
| Mark some sentence endings with a full stop. | 1Wp1 | 68 | 71 | |
| Compose and write a simple sentence with a capital letter and a full stop. | 1Wp2 | 55, 63 | 67 | |
| Write sentence-like structures which may be joined by *and*. | 1Wp3 | 60, 66 | 62, 67 | 27 |
| **Speaking and listening** | | | | |
| Speak clearly and choose words carefully to express feelings and ideas when speaking of matters of immediate interest. | 1SL1 | 56 | 60 | |
| Speak confidently to a group to share an experience. | 1SL5 | 57 | 60 | |
| Take turns in speaking. | 1SL6 | 52 | 58 | |
| Listen to others and respond appropriately. | 1SL7 | 68 | 71 | |
| Engage in imaginative play, enacting simple characters or situations. | 1SL9 | 56 | 60 | |

# The lion and the mouse

Pages 52–55

Pages 24–25

## Objectives

- Anticipate what happens next in a story. (1Ri1)
- Read a range of common words on sight. (1R10)
- Demonstrate an understanding that one spoken word corresponds with one written word. (1R07)
- Join in with reading familiar, simple stories and poems. (1R08)
- Blend to read, and segment to spell, words with final and initial adjacent consonants, e.g. *b-l, n-d.* (1R05)

## Starter

- Inform the learners that the next part of their Learner's book has 'traditional stories'. Can partners remind each other what a story is? (Something made up.) Explain that a traditional story is usually old and uses some familiar story language.

- Ask: *What traditional stories do we know?* Share titles, e.g. 'Cinderella', 'Little Red Riding Hood' and famous old tales from your culture. Choose one that the learners know. Ask them to tell a partner the starting words they would use when telling that story. How many learners begin *Once upon a time…?* Agree that this is a likely start for a traditional story.

- Direct the learners to page 52 of the Learner's book. Read the page aloud (only this page) as the learners follow. Read it again, the learners placing a finger under the words as they are read. Pause occasionally before short, common words for the learners to read them. Finally, read together, the learners joining in as much as possible.

- Use partner and then class discussion to talk about what has happened so far in the story. Clear up any misunderstandings.

## Activity notes and answers

**Discuss a traditional story.** Direct the learners to the *Talk Partners* box on page 52 of the Learner's book. Read it aloud, explaining that each partner takes a turn asking and answering the questions. Share answers as a class about what may happen next. Encourage the learners to have confidence in their opinions. Emphasise that a story is made up, so the writer can make anything happen.

1. **Read along with the story.** Direct the learners to page 53 of the Learner's book. Read the page aloud. As with page 52, ask the learners to follow, placing a finger under the words, and to read parts with you. Choose 'sleep' (sentence 1) as a word to pause before and read with the learners.

   Write **s l ee p** on the board. Explain that these are the separate graphemes (written forms) for the phonemes in 'sleep'. Underline the first two letters. Choose one learner to stand in front of the class holding the grapheme 's' and another to hold 'l'. Begin with them clearly apart and ask the class to say their phonemes from left to right. Ask them to move close together so that one grapheme's sound runs smoothly into the next. Explain that this is called blending.

   Repeat the last exercise with the graphemes 'b' and 'r'; and 'g' and 'r'.

# *br, sl* and *gr*

**Helpful hints:** Read the Helpful hints box with the learners on page 54 of the Learner's book. Invite them to read the blends and words to a partner. Can they hear what is happening?

1. **Find words and blends.** Read the list of words to the learners. Put the learners into pairs to read the words together. Learners must write them and underline the first two letters. Can they tell each other what is special about the two letters? (They are blends.)

2. **Write blends.** Let the learners work with a partner as they use the pictures to decide on the words needed and the pair of letters to write. Encourage them to say the words aloud to each other before they write.
   **Answers:** a) bring    b) brush    c) grab    d) green    e) grass    f) slip    g) sleep

# Sight words

**Helpful hints:** Direct the learners to the Helpful hints box on page 55 of the Learner's book. Ask them to read the list of words aloud. Support them where necessary. Using pre-prepared cards, hold up individual words from the list for the learners to read aloud.

1. **Write the correct word.** Suggest partners read the sentences together and help each other choose the correct words from the bubble.
   **Answers:**
   a) Please give Ravi his hat.          b) The man went home.
   c) Please don't jump off the wall.          d) Do you need him to help you?

2. **Guess the word.** Explain that the learners must find the missing words. They have the first letter and the number of spaces to show how many letters are missing. Read the clues one at a time, partners then searching and helping each other. Remind them that a phoneme is a sound, and make the sound of the blend 'nt' for them to copy. Give further help by limiting the search to a small section of text each time.
   **Answers:** a) don't    b) his    c) off    d) went

## Success criteria ✓

While completing the activities, assess and record learners who can:

- anticipate what comes next in the story
- read a range of common words on sight
- join in with reading the story
- blend words to read, and segment to spell, words
- find examples of the blended consonants in a text, and write missing ones in a word.

## Workbook answers

**Blends**

1. a) string      b) clock
   c) drill        d) brush
   e) cloth      f) brick

## Further activities

- Learners complete Workbook pages 24–25.

- Give the learners this list of words to read to a partner and find in the story:
  *time, woke, nose, free, back, was, eat.*

- Ask partners to tell each other what they had expected to happen after reading half the story. What did they get right?

# Act it out

Pages 56–57

Page 26

## Objectives

- Read a range of common words on sight. (1R10)
- Engage in imaginative play, enacting simple characters or situations. (1SL9)
- Write a sequence of sentences retelling a familiar story or recounting an experience. (1Wt1)
- Speak confidently to a group to share an experience. (1SL5)
- Speak clearly and choose words carefully to express feelings and ideas when speaking of matters of immediate interest. (1SL1)

## Starter

- Remind the learners that stories have characters in them. Ask: *What are characters?* (People in the story.)
- Suggest that story characters, particularly in children's books, are not always real people. Ask: *What else could they be?* (Animals) Agree that animals are popular characters for children's storybooks. Show the learners some example books in the classroom.
- Select a story with an animal as a main character, making sure that the animal speaks. Ask: *How does the writer make this animal seem like a real person?* (The animal speaks, has feelings and perhaps does clever things.)
- Direct the learners to page 52 of the Learner's book. Ask: *Who are the main characters in this story?* (The lion and the mouse.) *How do they seem human?* (They speak and have ideas.)
- Divide the class in half: one half to be the lion and one to be the mouse. Explain that you will read the story but, when the animals speak, the learners will read their words for them. Read the story this way, indicating when each half should read and you (or a classroom assistant) offering support in a changed voice. Do this again, encouraging both groups to try to feel and sound like their character.

## Activity notes and answers

**Discuss character's feelings.** Direct the learners to the *Talk Partners* box on page 56 of the Learner's book. Read the box to the learners. Pause after each part for the partners to share ideas about the character's feelings and to choose and write an answer.

**Answers:** a) scared     b) amused     c) scared

1. **Make character masks and act the story.** Put the learners into groups of four to take parts. Make sure they know which character mask they are making. Ask: *Why will a mask be helpful?* (They will look and feel the part.)
2. **Think of a character's words.** Talk about what is happening in the pictures and who the speech bubbles are for. Suggest that for each speech bubble, the learners think about what the speaker is feeling and what they might say. Encourage them to say the speech aloud to a partner.

# Pictures

1. **Write a picture story of 'The lion and the mouse'.** Explain that the learners are going to make 'The lion and the mouse' into a picture story for younger readers. It needs six pictures and a sentence with each picture. Discuss what is in the pictures. Write helpful words on the board and some sentence starters (for example: The lion…; Hunters came…; The mouse…).

**Try this:** Point out the challenge box on Learner's book page 57. Explain what the learners must do. Point out that each learner will tell the story, in their own words, for two pictures. Put the learners into groups of three to choose two pictures each. They must practise actions and speech, and then put the whole story together. Remind them that the learner with the first picture says 'Once upon a time…'

## Success criteria ✓

While completing the activities, assess and record learners who can:

- engage in imaginative play, take the part of a character in a story and think of something for the story character to say
- create a sequence of pictures and write a sequence of sentences retelling the story of 'The lion and the mouse'
- tell a story to other learners.

## Workbook answers

**Common words practice**

1. a) his    b) help
   c) him    d) went
   e) off    f) don't
   g) came   h) has

2. The boy climbed up the wall. It was too high. "**Help!**" he called. **His** mother **came**. "**Don't** worry!" she said.

## Further activities

- Learners complete Workbook page 26.
- Take further the storytelling from *Try this* on Learner's book page 57 by asking each group to perform for another group. Encourage them to recognise that storytellers can tell a story differently.

**IT** Listen to some of Aesop's fables being read aloud on *www.bbc.co.uk/learning/schoolradio/subjects/english/aesops_fables*. Can the learners see similarities to 'The lion and the mouse'? Can they retell one of the new ones in a picture story?

- Read what the lion says at the end of the story. Do the learners know what the expression *being taught a lesson* means? (Someone understands they were wrong.) Can partners work out what the lion now realises he was wrong about? (Never needing help.) What does he now understand? (Even small people can help strong ones.)
- Choose new situations in the story, e.g. when the lion felt the mouse on his nose; when the mouse was nibbling at the ropes. Ask the learners to think of something for them to say each time and write it in a speech bubble.
- Read more of Aesop's fables to the learners (see Book list below).

## Assessment ideas

Ask the learners to make a new mask of the lion or the mouse. Let the learners hold the mask as you talk to them about situations in the story. Listen to them describe individually their feelings and say what they are thinking. Assess their ability to become a character.

## Book list

- *The Orchard Book of Aesop's Fables* by Michael Morpurgo (Orchard Books)

# The enormous turnip

 Pages 58–60

 Page 27

## Objectives

- Recognise story elements, e.g. beginning, middle and end. (1Rw2)
- Write sentence-like structures which may be joined by *and*. (1Wp3)

## Starter

- Remind the learners that a story divides into three parts. Ask: *What are the parts called?* Write 'beginning', 'middle' and 'end' on the board, but in random places. Ask the learners to help you list them in order.

- Ask: *Which story part is likely to be the longest?* Agree that the middle part is where most events happen, and so is likely to be the longest.

- Without looking at those pages, discuss the story 'The lion and the mouse', first in partner talk and then as a class. Ask: *What happens at the beginning? How does the story end? What events happen in the middle?* Afterwards, turn to pages 52–53 of the Learner's book to check how well they have remembered.

- Remind the learners that the stories in this part of the Learner's book are traditional stories. Do they remember what that means? (The stories are old and may use some similar language.) Explain that this type of story may also have a lesson to teach the reader (and a character). Ask: *What lesson does the lion and the reader learn in 'The lion and the mouse'?* (Even big strong people can be helped by small weak people.)

- Use the word *characters* when you talk about 'The lion and the mouse'. Question the learners about its meaning. Ask: *Who are the characters in 'The lion and the mouse'?* (A lion, a mouse, two hunters.) *Where is the story set?* Suggest that the setting (the place where the events happen) is probably the jungle.

- Direct the learners to page 58 of the Learner's book. Read pages 58–59, encouraging the learners first to follow words with their finger, and then to join in some of the reading. Pause after each numbered section for the learners to examine the details of the picture. Do the text and the pictures always give the same information?

## Activity notes and answers

# Beginning, middle and end

1. **Order story parts.** Read the instructions to the learners before partners read statements a, b and c together and decide on their order.

   **Answers:**
   b) Mr and Mrs Root planted seeds. **beginning**
   c) They tried to pull up the turnip. **middle**
   a) The turnip came out – POP! **end**

2. **Answer questions about character and setting.** Remind the learners what the characters and setting are in a story. Read each question separately. After each question, encourage partner discussion and turning back to Learner's book pages 58–59 to check the story text. Suggest that the learners write and draw their answers.

**Answers:**

a) Mr and Mrs Root.

b) They want pull up the last turnip.

c) A little mouse.

d) Six.

**Talk Partners**

**Learn from what happens in the story.** Direct the learners to the *Talk Partners* box on page 60 of the Learner's book. Remind the learners that traditional stories often have a lesson that you can learn from what happens in the story. Read the two answers for partners to talk about. Ask them to decide and write the letter and draw the picture for the one they choose.

## Success criteria

While completing the activities, assess and record learners who can:

- talk about the beginning, middle and end of a story
- talk about the characters, setting and events in a story
- write simple sentences to answer the questions.

**IT**

Visit *www.scholastic.co.uk* and search for 'Story Stage', a computer resource in which four learners may collaborate to retell 'The enormous turnip' and other traditional tales.

## Further activities

- Learners complete Workbook page 27.
- Give the learners three new statements about events in the story. Ask them to order them into beginning, middle, end.

  a) The chicken fell on the ground. **end**

  b) The turnip famer and his wife made a row of seeds. **beginning**

  c) The sheep, chicken and donkey helped. **middle**

- Give the learners new questions to answer about the story's characters, setting and events. They may record answers in pictures and writing.

  a) Who is the smallest character?

  b) What is different about the last turnip?

  c) What can no one do without help?

**Answers:**

a) The mouse.

b) It is enormous.

c) Pull out the enormous turnip.

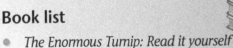

**Book list**

- *The Enormous Turnip: Read it yourself with Ladybird: Level 1* (Ladybird)

- Learners may be able to read the version of the story in the Book list independently.

## Assessment ideas

Discuss the learners' answers with them for activity 2 on Learner's book page 60.

Ask them to explain how they decided. Assess their understanding of the story and what is happening.

# Story words

Learner's book

Page 61

**Objectives**

- Talk about significant aspects of a story's language, e.g. repetitive refrain, rhyme, patterned language. (1Rw1)

## Starter

- Let one partner start telling the other the story 'The enormous turnip'. After half a minute, swap roles so the other partner starts telling the story, again from the beginning. Ask: *What words did you start with?*

- Listen to and write some answers on the board. For example: Once; Once upon a time; Long, long ago. Ask: *Did lots of you use the same words?*

- Direct the learners to page 52 of the Learner's book to read aloud the opening words. Do the same for page 58. What is surprising? (They are the same.) Remind the learners that both stories are traditional; they are likely to use similar language and repetition.

- Read aloud the second sentence on both pages 52 and 53 of the Learner's book. Ask: *Which words were repeated?* ('As he slept'.)

## Activity notes and answers

**Helpful hints:** Direct the learners to the Helpful hints box on page 61 of the Learner's book. Ask the learners to check if the starting words on the board match any of these. Ask: *Why does a writer repeat lines?* (To emphasise what is happening and help the reader to remember the story.)

1. **Find repetition.** With the learners, read aloud the groups of words they must look for in the story. Suggest partner work and counting twice before writing an answer.

   **Answers:**
   a) once
   b) four times
   c) three times
   d) three times

2. **Match stories and story starters.** Reading answers aloud to a partner will let the learners hear if their joined sentences make sense.

   **Answers:**
   a) *Once upon a time* there was a girl called Cinderella.
   b) *There once was* a giant who lived on a hill.
   c) *One day* Tom found a gold egg.

## Further activities

- Give reading groups a selection of short traditional stories. Ask the learners to write the titles and opening words. How many different ways of starting do they find?

- Extend activity 2 on Learner's book page 61 to thinking of the rest of the story for one opening line. In groups, the learners could create this story first orally, then in pictures and finally with sentences.

**Success criteria** ✓

While completing the activities, assess and record learners who can:

- find the repeated phrases in the story.

# Retelling a story

Pages 62–63

Pages 28–29

## Objectives

- Recognise story elements, e.g. beginning, middle and end. (1Rw2)
- Retell stories, with some appropriate use of story language. (1R13)
- Talk about significant aspects of a story's language, e.g. repetitive refrain, rhyme, patterned language. (1Rw1)
- Compose and write a simple sentence with a capital letter and a full stop. (1Wp2)

## Starter

- Explain to the learners that there is a difference between telling and reading a story. Telling relies on the voice and the words to keep the listener interested. Point out that the storyteller's language needs to help the listener remember what happens in the story.

- Ask: *What are useful starting words?* Agree that 'Once upon a time' is familiar and lets listeners know that a story is starting. *What makes what is happening in the story easier to understand and remember?* (Repetition)

- Suggest that telling a story helps us to get ready for writing. It is a way to try out how the words sound and, by testing them on a partner, we can find out if they will keep people interested.

- Direct the learners to page 58 of the Learner's book and reread the story 'The enormous turnip'.

## Activity notes and answers

**Talk Partners**

**Retell a story.** Direct the learners to the *Talk Partners* box on page 62 of the Learner's book. Check the learners can read the picture labels. Read a) and b) together. Explain that partners should tell the story of 'The enormous turnip' to each other, making sure that they include lines a) and b). Ask: *Will you say each set of words just once?* ('but she could not pull up the turnip' would be effective words to repeat.) *Will you tell each other the whole story?* (They may decide to tell half each.)

# Story language

1. **Write what characters are saying.** Discuss what is happening in the pictures in activity 1 on page 63 of the Learner's book. Point out who the speech bubble is next to. Put the learners into groups to act each scene and think what they would say as that character in that situation. Suggest they try saying it aloud before writing it. Write a bank of useful words on the board. Support individual learners by listening to their sentences and writing words for them to copy.

2. **Write a familiar story.** Read the instructions aloud as the learners follow. Remind them that they have already told this story to a partner; now they must write it for a reader. Read points a) to d), clearing up any confusion. Point out examples of full stops and capital letters in the story text, and explain that they should choose the words from one of their speech bubbles to use. They must decide on the content of their four pictures carefully. Remind them that pages 58–59 of the Learner's book will provide the spelling of many words they need. Offer support with any other words that give spelling problems.

### Success criteria ✓

While completing the activities, assess and record learners who can:

- retell stories in their own words, using the type of language and repetition that is appropriate for a traditional story.

### Workbook answers

**Chicken Licken questions**

1. a) A rock falls on Foxy Loxy. **End**
   b) An acorn falls on Chicken Licken. **Beginning**
   c) Chicken Licken finds her friends. **Middle**

2. a) four times
   b) three times
   c) four times

3. a) No
   b) Because he is going to eat the birds.

### Further activities

- Learners read Workbook page 28 and complete Workbook page 29.
- Follow up the *Talk Partner* work on page 62 of the Learner's book by the learners retelling the story to a larger group.
- Read some traditional fairy tales from around the world with the learners (see Book list below).

### Book list

- *The Fabrics of Fairy Tale: Stories spun from far and wide* retold by Tanya Robyn Batt (Barefoot Books)

# The paintbrush

*Learner's book*

Pages 64–66

*Workbook*

Page 30

## Objectives

- Pause at full stops when reading. (1R17)
- Talk about events in a story and make simple inferences about characters and events to show understanding. (1Ri2)
- Retell stories, with some appropriate use of story language. (1R13)
- Write sentence-like structures which may be joined by *and*. (1Wp3)

## Starter

- Ask the learners what they should see at the end of a sentence. (A full stop.) How will they recognise one when reading? It starts with a capital letter and ends with a full stop.

- Invite the learners to close their eyes as you read this aloud: *It was a hot day. We went for a swim.* Read it a few times, making your pause at the first full stop obvious. Could the learners tell there were two sentences? What happened to your voice? (You paused between the sentences.)

- Write your text this way on the board: *it was a hot day we went for a swim* without capital letters or full stops. Can the learners help you put them in? Suggest partners read the words to each other as they decide where to end one sentence and begin the second one. Share answers and add the capital letters and full stops to the board.

- Write *and* on the board. Explain that *and* is a very useful word. Can the learners suggest why? (It can join one set of words to another.)

- Write two sentences on the board: *Mr Root was big. Mr Root was strong.* What do the learners notice about the first three words in both sentences? (They are the same.) Suggest it would be easier to join the sentences with *and*; then you could just write everything once in one sentence. Let partners discuss what to write. Share ideas and write the new, joined sentence on the board: *Mr Root was big and strong.*

## Activity notes and answers

1. **Read aloud.** Direct the learners to page 64 of the Learner's book. Read the page aloud (only this page) as the learners follow. Read it again, the learners placing a finger under the words as they are read. Finally, read together, the learners joining in as much as possible.

**Talk Partners**

**Discuss and memorise a story.** Direct the learners to the *Talk Partners* box on page 65 of the Learner's book. Remind the learners of where the story stopped on page 64. Move to page 65 and read it aloud as the learners follow. Read it again, the learners placing a finger under the words as they are read. Pause before some words for the learners to read. Suggest the partners take turns saying what happens. The listener must be ready to help. Move among partners, prompting memories and correcting misunderstandings of the story.

# Using *and*

## Activity notes and answers

1.  **Answer questions about the story.** Explain that all these questions are about what happens in the story. Read the first question aloud as the learners follow. Let partners tell each other the answer, then invite an answer from an individual learner. Agree on what is correct and together construct an oral sentence. Do all the questions in this way, directing the learners to places in the story that will help them.

    **Answers:**
    a)  The two main characters are Ma Liang and the mean, rich man.
    b)  Ma Liang loved to draw.
    c)  He feels surprised and happy. (Accept learners' ideas.)
    d)  He captures Ma Liang to make him draw gold for him.
    e)  He is drowned.

2.  **Use *and* to join sentences.** Remind the learners that *and* can join sentences and save words. Repeat your example in the Starter. Read aloud the pairs of sentences in activity 2 on page 66 of the Learner's book. Let partners read them to each other before they decide and write the new sentence. Support them by checking they are not going to write words twice.

    **Answers:**
    a)  The day was hot and sunny.
    b)  I have one book and pen.
    c)  I will have a wash and go to bed.
    d)  He went to help Tom and Tim.
    e)  The mouse was brave and clever.

3.  **Add information with *and*.** Explain that *and* can add new information to a sentence. Read the unfinished sentences aloud for the learners to copy and finish as they choose.

    **Possible answers:**
    a)  I like bread and honey.
    b)  The bird sings and flies.
    c)  The bus is red and white.
    d)  At school, we read and write.

### Success criteria ✔

While completing the activities, assess and record learners who can:

- pause at full stops when reading
- talk about what happens in the story and understand what the characters do
- retell the story using simple sentences.

IT  Use the BBC school radio site *www.bbc.co.uk/learning/schoolradio/ subjects/english/hans_christian_andersen /tales* for the learners to listen to some of Andersen's fairy tales.

## Further activities

- Learners use the pictures on Workbook page 30 to tell someone the story of *Chicken Licken*.
- Return to activity 1 on page 66 of the Learner's book. Provide the first two or three written words of each answer for the learners to copy and complete.
- Read the story on Learner's book pages 64–65 aloud, the learners miming what is happening. At points, ask the learners to freeze in character. Bring individuals to life to question, in character, what they are doing or feeling.

# More blends

 Learner's book
Page 67

## Objectives

- Form letters correctly. (1W02)
- Blend to read, and segment to spell, words with final and initial adjacent consonants, e.g. *b-l, n-d.* (1R05)

## Starter

- Choose one learner to stand in front of the class holding the grapheme 's' and another to hold 'l'. Place both learners facing the class, but standing clearly apart. Ask the class to say their sounds from left to right. Move the learners at the front, and their cards, close together. Ask the class to say their sounds again, this time one immediately after the other so that one grapheme's sound runs smoothly into the next. Explain that this is called blending.

- Repeat the last exercise with the graphemes 'b' and 'r', and 'g' and 'r'. Invite different learners to hold cards and demonstrate blending by moving the cards together.

- Write this on the board: *When the weather brings ice and snow, it is great fun to slide.* Challenge the learners to spot three words with the blends you have been making. Underline the words and put the blends in bold. (**br**ing, **gr**eat, **sl**ide.)

- Display some lower case letters: e, i, o, c, f, g, k, l, n, p. For each, point out its starting point. Stand with your back to the learners, your finger forming the letter in the air with the index finger of your writing hand. Ask the learners to copy by writing in the air. If another adult is available to model letter formation, move among the learners, checking and adjusting their movements.

- Direct the learners to pages 64–65 of the Learner's book and reread the whole of the story 'The paintbrush'.

## Activity notes and answers

1. **Find words containing blends.** Point out the three blends in bold font. Ask the learners to make their sounds. Suggest they work with a partner as they search the story for words containing them.

   **Answers:**
   a) slept
   b) floor
   c) brush

2. **Write blends.** Remind the learners about starting points in the letters. Suggest partners watch you and then each other, finger-trace letter shapes and air-write before they write the blends in their books.

3. **Practise writing.** Read the instructions to the learners. Read the list of words together. Ask the learners to check which letters in the words they have most difficulty writing. They should spend longer tracing these letter shapes and air-writing them. After writing a word once, encourage partners to help each other look for letters they need to improve the next time. They should also think about their pencil grip. Is it a comfortable one? Does it allow them to move the pencil well?

## Success criteria ✓

While completing the activities, assess and record learners who can:

- form letters correctly
- find words that contain blends.

## Further activities

- Provide more words for handwriting practice similar to activity 3 on Learner's book page 67. Use words containing blends, e.g. *flag, slip, clap*.

- Ask the learners to read 'The lion and the mouse' on pages 52–53 of the Learner's book. What words can they find beginning with the blends **sl**, **br** and **gr**?

  **sl**: four words (sleeping, sleepy, sleep, slept)

  **br**: one word (brave)

  **gr**: two words (great, grin)

 **IT** Listen to or read stories from around the world in a range of different languages at *www.worldstories.org.uk*.

## Assessment ideas

Provide new written words for the learners to look at and write: *flock, grip, bring*. Watch as they trace the shapes and do air-writing. As they write on paper, do they continue to form letters correctly?

# Writing a sentence

Pages 68–69

Page 31

**Objectives**

● Mark some sentence endings with a full stop. (1Wp1)
● Write simple storybooks with sentences to caption pictures. (1Wa1)
● Listen to others and respond appropriately. (1SL7)

## Starter

● Show the learners a selection of simple storybooks for children of their age. Point out that the books have pictures and writing. Open a book at a double spread of a picture and accompanying text. Ask: *What does the writing have to do with the picture?* Suggest that the words tell the reader what is happening in the story; the picture shows that.

● Ask the learners to think about a storybook they enjoy. Ask: *Do you think the words and the pictures are both important parts of the book? Do they make the book easier to understand?* Suggest that both parts are important in children's books.

● Hold up your book again. Ask how the writing in a book is divided up. Prompt the learners into using the word *sentence*. Can they explain to their partner what a sentence is? Agree that it is a group of words that makes sense. Point to a page and ask: *Can you see any sentences? How can you recognise them?* Remind the learners that a sentence starts with a capital letter and ends with a full stop.

● Direct the learners to pages 64–65 of the Learner's book and read aloud the whole of the story 'The paintbrush'.

## Activity notes and answers

Talk Partners

**Make sentences to go with the pictures.** Direct the learners to the *Talk Partners* box on page 68 of the Learner's book. Talk about the pictures. Make sure that the learners know which part of the story each picture refers to. Clear up any possible confusion by asking about each picture in turn.

Suggest that partners discuss each picture. They must think of a sentence to go with each one. Encourage them to keep the sentences short.

1. **Write sentences for pictures.** Put the same partners to work together as in the *Talk Partners* activity: they can remind each other of their sentences. Remind them to put sounds together as they spell words. The story on pages 64–65 of the Learner's book will also help them with some of the words.

   **Possible sentences:**
   a) Ma Liang found a paintbrush by his bed.
   b) He used it to draw food and water.
   c) The rich man captured Ma Liang.
   d) Ma Liang drew a large wave.

# Making a book

1. **Write a storybook.** Ask the learners if they have ever written a book. What did they use? How did they put the pages together? Point out the pictures on page 69 of the Learner's book that show how to make a mini-book. Show the learners one that you have already prepared. Give everyone a piece of paper and take the learners slowly through the folding and cutting process. Always demonstrate first. Encourage partner support and be aware of less-confident learners. Read instructions c) and d) aloud and remind the learners to use the sentences they have already written. They may copy the pictures from page 68 of the Learner's book or draw new ones of their own. Remind them to have a picture on one page and a sentence on the page opposite.

**What have I learnt?** Suggest partners read through this box together. Did they both do all these things? Have they forgotten any full stops?

**Success criteria**

While completing the activities, assess and record learners who can:

- use a full stop at the end of a sentence
- create a storybook with pictures and sentences.

 **IT** You may wish to access *www.scholastic.co.uk* on the internet. The website's 'We are Writers' section helps the learners use computers to write and print their stories in a published book.

## Further activities

- Put the learners into groups so that they can read one another's books. Encourage positive feedback in comments to one another: for example, enjoyment of the final picture because of the look on the rich man's face.
- Follow the same process as the learners reread 'The lion and the mouse'. They can decide on four pictures and sentences, and make and write their own storybook for it.

## Assessment ideas

- Make an assessment sheet modelled on the *What have I learnt?* box. Add to the checklist: *wrote sentences that matched my pictures.* Create a space on the sheet for the learners to write (or tell you what to write) how they would do better next time.
- Learners complete the Self-assessment table on page 31 of the Workbook.

# Unit 5 Reports and dictionaries

## Objectives Overview

| Learning Objective | Objective Code | Learner's book Activities | Teacher's pack Activities | Workbook Activities |
|---|---|---|---|---|
| **Reading** | | | | |
| Know the name of and most common sound associated with every letter in the English alphabet. | 1R02 | 84 | 89 | |
| Use knowledge of sounds to read and write single syllable words with short vowels. | 1R04 | 75 | 79 | |
| Blend to read, and segment to spell, words with final and initial adjacent consonants, e.g. *b-l, n-d.* | 1R05 | 83 | 87 | |
| Use phonic knowledge to read decodable words and to attempt to sound out some elements of unfamiliar words. | 1R06 | 72, 73, 76, 77 | 77, 81 | |
| Read a range of common words on sight. | 1R10 | 76, 77 | 81 | 35 |
| Enjoy reading and listening to a range of books, drawing on background information and vocabulary provided. | 1R11 | 71 | 74 | |
| Read aloud independently from simple books. | 1R16 | 72, 73 | 77 | |
| Read labels, lists and captions to find information. | 1Rx1 | 79 | 83 | |
| Show awareness that texts for different purposes look different, e.g. use of photographs, diagrams. | 1Rv1 | 70, 71, 72, 73, 82 | 74, 77, 87 | 32, 33 |
| Know the parts of a book, e.g. title page, contents. | 1Rv2 | 70, 74, 79 | 74, 81, 83 | 36 |
| **Writing** | | | | |
| Form letters correctly. | 1W02 | 79 | 83 | |
| Use knowledge of sounds to write simple regular words, and to attempt other words including when writing simple sentences dictated by the teacher from memory. | 1W04 | 75 | 79 | |
| Read own writing aloud and talk about it. | 1W05 | 81 | 85 | |
| Record answers to questions, e.g. as lists, charts. | 1Wa3 | 80 | 85 | |
| Write for a purpose using some basic features of text type. | 1Wa5 | 80, 84 | 85 | 38 |
| Compose and write a simple sentence with a capital letter and a full stop. | 1Wp2 | 75 | 79 | 34 |
| Spell familiar common words accurately, drawing on sight vocabulary. | 1Ws2 | 79 | 83 | |
| **Speaking and listening** | | | | |
| Speak clearly and choose words carefully to express feelings and ideas when speaking of matters of immediate interest. | 1SL1 | 75, 80 | 85 | |
| Answer questions and explain further when asked. | 1SL4 | 74, 85 | 89 | |

# Different books

Learner's book
Pages 70–71

Workbook
Page 32

## Objectives

- Know the parts of a book, e.g. title page, contents. (1Rv2)
- Show awareness that texts for different purposes look different, e.g. use of photographs, diagrams. (1Rv1)
- Enjoy reading and listening to a range of books, drawing on background information and vocabulary provided. (1R11)

## Starter

- Have an alphabet poster on display and collect together some children's books. Show the learners your random box or piles of books. Explain that you are sorting the books into two sections: fiction and non-fiction. Remind them that fiction is about made-up things, stories.

- Write *non-fiction* on the board. Can the learners work out what non-fiction books must be? (Books that tells us real things, facts.) Suggest that a book's cover and title are often clues to whether a book is fiction or non-fiction. Write two book titles on the board:
  - o  Teddy in Lollipop Land
  - o  Farm animals

- Put the children into pairs with voting cards, one saying fiction, one non-fiction. Read the titles on the board aloud. Let partners discuss what the books may be about. Do they sound like stories or facts? Agree that 'Teddy in Lollipop Land' is fiction; 'Farm animals' is non-fiction.

- Draw attention to the unit heading: *Reports and dictionaries* on page 70 of the Learner's book. Hold up a dictionary. Explain that it has words arranged in the same order as the alphabet. (Point to your classroom alphabet.) Tell the learners that you want to check the word *tiger*. Ask: *What sound starts the word?* (t) *What letter makes that sound?* ('t') *Where is that letter in the alphabet?* (Near the end.) Demonstrate opening the dictionary near the end, and finding *tiger*. Show and read the entry. Ask: *How has the dictionary helped me?* (It has told you what a tiger is and how to spell the word.)

- Return to the other part of the unit heading: *Reports*. Explain that a report is a piece of text that gives facts on a subject. It is written in sentences and is set out clearly to help the reader find information. Point out the second Helpful hints box on page 70 of the Learner's book.

- Show an example page from one of your non-fiction books. Draw attention to a heading, and a picture with a caption. Ask: *Why is the caption useful?* (It says what the picture is about.) *What does the heading mean?* (There is information about it underneath.)

- Show the learners the contents page of your book. What is written? (A list dividing up the information in the book and telling the readers the page numbers to turn to.)

- Direct the learners to the second Helpful hints box on page 70 of the Learner's book. Read the explanations and explore the examples with them.

## Activity notes and answers

1. **Sort books by their covers.** Read the instruction and the book titles aloud. Put the learners into pairs to discuss the book covers.

   **Answers:**
   a) fiction 'Pirate adventure'
   b) non-fiction 'Big cats'
   c) non-fiction 'Rivers'
   d) fiction 'Alice in Wonderland'

# Report books

1. **Find features inside a report book.** Read aloud and explain what the learners have to do. Put them into pairs with a non-fiction book of a suitable level. Ask them to find page numbers for the answers for a). For b) the answers may be written in a word or a sentence.

2. **Sort books.** Read aloud and explain the instructions. Put the learners into pairs. Give them a mixed collection of classroom books to sort into fiction and non-fiction. Check each pair's results. For b) give each learner a chance to sort books individually and to explain their choices to a partner. Move around the classroom, listening to reasons.

3. **Match photographs and captions.** Read the activity aloud with the class. Less-confident readers may prefer to complete the activity with a partner.

   **Answers:**
   a) Baby cats like to play.
   b) Lions sleep in the day.
   c) Tigers have stripes.

### Success criteria ✓

While completing the activities, assess and record learners who can:

● recognise the different parts of a non-fiction book
● decide which books they want to read.

 IT

Photograph four animals. Upload the photographs on to your computer. Write four captions for the learners to match correctly.

### Workbook answers

**Fiction or non-fiction?**

1. a) fiction
   b) fiction
   c) non-fiction
   d) non-fiction

2. a) fiction
   b) non-fiction
   c) non-fiction
   d) fiction

## Further activities

- Learners complete Workbook page 32.
- Suggest the learners write new captions for the photographs in activity 3 on Learner's book page 71.
- Put the learners into pairs with a simple dictionary. Read out the names of some jungle animals, for example: *cheetah, leopard, monkey, gorilla*. Ask: *What letter starts the word?*
- Ask the learners to create a contents page for a non-fiction book with the title 'Farm animals'.
- Encourage the learners to browse through non-fiction books on their own (see Book list below for an example).

### Assessment ideas

Invite the learners to tell you what fiction and non-fiction books are. Give them a mixture of books to label correctly as fiction or non-fiction.

### Book list

- *Animals and the Environment* (First Step Non-fiction Ecology) by Jennifer Boothroyd (Lerner Books)

# Lego

Pages 72–73

Page 33

## Objectives

- Read aloud independently from simple books. (1R16)
- Show awareness that different texts for different purposes look different, e.g. use of photographs, diagrams. (1Rv1)
- Use phonic knowledge to read decodable words and to attempt to sound out some elements of unfamiliar words. (1R06)

## Starter

- Write a simple, familiar word on the board, such as *can*. Ask the learners to read it aloud. Put the learners into pairs to share ideas on how they knew how to read it.

- Emphasise the importance of phonics, the use of sounds, when we read. Erase the word and write it again as separate graphemes: 'c' 'a' 'n'. Demonstrate finger-tracking under the graphemes of the word from left to write while saying the sounds. After saying the sounds one at a time, return the index finger to under the first grapheme and run the finger under the whole word, while saying the whole blended word.

- Ask the learners to write the word *can* in their books. Repeat the finger-tracking and blending, the learners joining in with you.

- Write a new word on the board: can the learners help you say the sounds and then the word as you finger-track and blend? Do this with other familiar words, for example: *big, got, and, just*. Invite pairs of learners to come to the board and demonstrate using finger-tracking as they decode the word.

- Explain that using phonics in this way can help them read new words. Write *van* on the board for them to copy. Put the learners into pairs to finger-track and read the word to each other. Can the class read the word aloud? Explain its meaning.

- Remind the learners that in this section of the Learner's book they are reading non-fiction texts. Ask: *What are non-fiction books?* (Books that tell us facts.)

- Direct the learners to pages 72–73 of the Learner's book. Invite them to look at the pages. Ask: *What do you notice about the way the pages are set out? What is different from your storybook?* (Headings and photographs.) Ask the learners to identify examples of headings.

- Read pages 72–73 of the Learner's book aloud as the learners follow, placing a finger under the words as they are read. Finally, read together, the learners joining in as much as possible.

## Activity notes and answers

1. **Read independently.** Suggest that the learners read pages 72–73 of the Learner's book aloud quietly to themselves until they are confident. Then put them into pairs to read to a partner. Can they help each other decode unfamiliar words?

### Success criteria

While completing the activities, assess and record learners who can:

- read the text aloud by themselves
- identify the differences between a fiction and non-fiction text.

 **IT** Let the learners explore the website for Malaysia's Legoland at *www.legoland.com.my.* Show them the photograph of visitors at the entrance and ask them to think of and write a caption.

## Further activities

- Learners complete Workbook page 33.
- Display some non-fiction books of an appropriate reading level. These could include books about Lego (see Book list below). Let partners choose a book and take turns reading it to each other.
- Suggest partners choose sections of the text on pages 72–73 of the Learner's book to read to each other. Can the listening partner hear the words clearly? Is the reader pausing at full stops?
- Challenge the learners to add their own heading to the non-fiction text about Lego on Learner's book pages 72–73.

### Book list

- *The Lego Ideas Book* by Daniel Lipkowitz (Dorling Kindersley)

### Workbook answers

**How books look**

1. a) tells me something (non-fiction)

   I can see:
   c) picture
   d) caption
   e) main heading
   f) small heading

2. a) This book is about elephants.
   b) The photograph shows elephants walking.
   c) The caption says elephants are herbivores.
   d) The small heading says Diet.

# Who, what, where or when?

Pages 74–75

Page 34

## Objectives

- Use knowledge of sounds to read and write single syllable words with short vowels. (1R04)
- Compose and write a simple sentence with a capital letter and a full stop. (1Wp2)

## Starter

- Remind the learners that they are reading non-fiction texts in this section of the Learner's book. Ask: *What are non-fiction books?* (Books that tell us facts.) *What are the facts about?* Agree that the facts may be about any subject.

- Show the learners a selection of classroom non-fiction books. Make sure that your books cover a range of topics with a focus on people, things, places or time. Draw the learners' attention to the subheading at the top of page 74 of the Learner's book. Explain that these are all question words. Deal with each question word in turn, discussing the type of answer it produces. *Who?* gives people; *What?* gives things; *Where?* gives places; *When?* gives time. Examine the title of each of your non-fiction books. Ask: *Which question word does it probably answer?*

- Suggest that using sounds (phonics) will help the learners spell correctly. Demonstrate the process of encoding (segmenting). Say the word *ships* slowly. Tally the sounds of the words on the thumb and fingers of your left hand and write down graphemes, which are code for each sound you have tallied, to spell the word: 'sh' 'i' 'p' 's'. Say another word, *fish*, for the learners to encode with you.

- Remind the learners that text is written in sentences. Direct the learners to pages 72–73 of the Learner's book. Can they see a sentence easily to show their partner? How did they find a sentence so quickly? Remind the learners that a sentence starts with a capital letter and ends with a full stop.

- Read pages 72–73 of the Learner's book aloud. Let the learners join in. Draw attention to some sentences that use *and*. Emphasise that *and* is a useful way to join information together.

## Activity notes and answers

**True or false.** Direct the learners to the *Talk Partners* box on page 74 of the Learner's book. Remind the learners that pages 72–73 of the Learner's book provide facts. Emphasise the need to read carefully to understand these facts. Suggest reading the statements on page 74 of the Learner's book together, finding the correct part of the text on pages 72–73 and deciding whether they are true or false.

**Answers:** a) true    b) false    c) false    d) true

1. **Search a text.** Remind the learners what a caption and heading are. (A caption tells you about a picture; a heading tells you what the words below will be about.) Let the learners work independently or with partner support.

   **Example answers:**
   a) the picture of the spaceship
   b) This spaceship used five million bricks.
   c) Largest model

# My favourite toy

1.  **Draw pictures for non-fiction books.** Have a preliminary class discussion about favourite toys. Put the learners into pairs to do the activity. Remind them to use segmenting (encoding) to help them spell words.

    **Example answers:**
    a) Koala
    b) cuddly, soft

**Share and discuss a picture of a favourite toy.** Direct the learners to the *Talk Partners* box on page 75 of the Learner's book. Point out the question words: *who, when, what*. The learners must tell their partners facts that give this information. Suggest that each partner needs to say three sentences. Encourage clear speaking, eye contact and careful listening.

2.  **Write non-fiction sentences.** Read the activity aloud to the learners. Remind them that their answers in activity 1 can help them. If necessary, provide the support of a sentence framework:

    My _____ is _____ and _____ .

**Try this:** Let more-confident writers progress to this. Encourage them to think about what new information they can tell about their toy.

## Further activities

- Learners complete Workbook page 34.
- Direct the learners to the *Talk Partners* box on page 75 of the Learner's book to write their answers.
- Ask the learners to write a sentence saying where they play with their toy.
- Give the learners two sentences without full stops and capital letters. Can they copy them out correctly?

  For example:

  *building with plastic bricks is fun you can make anything you like*

  **Answer:**

  *Building with plastic bricks is fun. You can make anything you like.*

## Success criteria

While completing the activities, assess and record learners who can:

- use knowledge of sounds (phonics) to write words
- write a simple sentence with a capital letter and a full stop.

## Assessment ideas

Give the learners five unpunctuated sentences to correct with capital letters and full stops.

a) we have non-fiction books in our classroom
b) there is one book about toys
c) the book does not tell you about Lego
d) it needs a new heading and picture
e) i will take a photograph of my Lego car

# Animals

Pages 76–78

Page 35

## Objectives

- Use phonic knowledge to read decodable words and to attempt to sound out some elements of unfamiliar words. (1R06)
- Read a range of common words on sight. (1R10)
- Know the parts of a book, e.g. title page, contents. (1Rv2)

## Starter

- Write 'that' on the board. Ask the learners to read it to a partner. Can they explain to each other how they knew how to read it?  Suggest that they probably know from seeing the word in their reading books.

- Suggest that they may be able to read words they are not used to seeing by using the word's sounds (phonics). Demonstrate decoding (blending) by writing 'ship' on the board. Explain that you are going to say its sounds and blend them together. Write the word again, its graphemes separated like this: 'sh' 'i' 'p'. Finger-track under the graphemes from left to write while saying the sounds. After saying the sounds one at a time, return your index finger to under the first grapheme and run it under the whole word, while saying the whole blended word.

- Ask the learners to write 'ship' in their books. Repeat the finger-tracking and blending, the learners joining in with you.

- Write different words containing blends on the board, for example: 'plot', 'mind', 'plan', 'find', 'flat'. Ask the learners to join in as you blend sounds to read the whole word. Invite pairs of learners to come to the board and demonstrate finger-tracking as you all blend the sounds so you can hear the whole word.

- Remind the learners that they are reading non-fiction texts in this section of the Learner's book. Direct them to pages 76–77 of the Learner's book. Ask: *Does this look like a non-fiction text? Why?* Comment on the headings, pictures, captions and table. Explain that the text is a report on animal homes. Point out that the information can be read in any order.

## Activity notes and answers

**Talk Partners**

**Read a non-fiction page.** Put the learners into pairs and direct them to the *Talk Partners* box on page 76 of the Learner's book. Ask them to read the page together, watching for words they know and using phonics and blending for others. Encourage them to move on in the text rather than staying stuck on one word; the word may become obvious from the meaning of the sentence. For less-confident readers, create a larger group or provide adult support. Finally, read the page aloud as the learners follow.

# Finding information

1.  **Find information.** Direct the learners to page 77 of the Learner's book. Follow the same process as before, partners reading the text together, noticing which words they know how to read and decoding others with phonics. Then read the page aloud as the learners follow. Point out that the text on pages 76–77 does not need to be written or read in any particular order. Put the learners into pairs to read their selected part to each other. Can they explain why they chose it? Ask them to write the heading of their chosen part.

Talk Partners

**Find information.** Direct the learners to the *Talk Partners* box on page 78 of the Learner's book. Suggest that learners take turns pointing to parts of the text. Their partners must agree with their choice.

**Answers:**
a)  Polar bear dens    b)  Ant colony    c)  Weaver bird nests    d)  Beaver lodges

**Helpful hints:** Point out the box on page 78 of the Learner's book and read it together.

2.  **Check facts in the text.** Remind the learners of the need to check what the texts says. Point out that headings will help them find the facts. After writing their answers, they should compare results with a partner. If they disagree, they both need to check the text again.

    **Answers:** a) true    b) false    c) true    d) false    e) false

## Success criteria ✓

While completing the activities, assess and record learners who can:

*   use phonics to read some unknown words
*   read a range of common words on sight
*   recognise the parts of a book.

## Workbook answers

**Common words crossword**

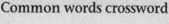

|   |   |   |   |   | ⁵s |   |   |   |
|---|---|---|---|---|---|---|---|---|
|   |   | ⁴a | b | o | u | ⁶t |   |   |
| ¹o | u | ²t |   |   | m |   | h |   |
|   |   | ³h | e | r | e |   | e |   |
|   |   | e |   |   |   |   | i |   |
|   |   | m |   |   | ⁷v | e | r | y |

## Further activities

*   Learners complete Workbook page 35.
*   Return to activity 2 on page 78 of the Learner's book. Ask the learners to write three more statements that the text on pages 76–77 tells them are true.
*   Put the learners into pairs to point out to each other the part of the text on Learner's book pages 76–77 that tells them about: a) swimming underwater; b) making a pile of earth; c) making a den in snow.
*   Ask the learners to list from the text on Learner's book pages 76–77: a) four words they knew how to read; b) four words that they worked out using phonics. Suggest talking to a partner first and limit the amount of text being looked at.

# Tables

Learner's book  Page 79

Workbook  Page 36

Learner's book Page 79
Workbook Page 36

## Objectives

- Form letters correctly. (1W02)
- Know the parts of a book, e.g. title page, contents. (1Rv2)
- Spell familiar common words accurately, drawing on sight vocabulary. (1Ws2)

## Starter

- Display lower case letters. For each, point out its starting point. Stand with your back to the learners, your finger forming the letter in the air with the index finger of your writing hand. Ask the learners to copy by writing in the air. If another adult is available to model letter formation, move among the learners, checking and adjusting their movements.

- Direct the learners to pages 76–77 of the Learner's book. Read the text aloud as the learners follow. Ask: *Is this a fiction or non-fiction text?* (Non-fiction.) *What helps you know just by looking at the text?* Let partners share views before you share ideas as a class. Point out that the headings, pictures and captions all indicate that it is a non-fiction text.

- Invite the learners to look again at pages 76–77 of the Learner's book. Ask: *What is unusual in this text?* (The table on page 77.) Explain that a table is a way to display information. A table is made up of columns and rows. Ask: *What information is shown in this table?* (The names of animals' homes.)

- Make sure that the learners understand the difference between a column and a row. Demonstrate on the board that a column is a list going downwards; a row is a list going across the page.

- Direct the learners to the Helpful hints box on page 79 of the Learner's book. Read it aloud and demonstrate moving down a column and across a row with a finger.

- Look together at the table on page 77 of the Learner's book. Ask: *What does the first column on the left list?* (The animals.) *What does each row tell you?* (Where the animals live.)

## Activity notes and answers

1. **Use a table.** Put the learners into pairs to read the activity. Read it together as a class and clear up any confusion. Emphasise that the learners must use the table to find their answers. Demonstrate moving your finger down a column and along a row.

   **Answers:**
   a) nest
   b) beaver
   c) den
   d) ants

**Writing presentation:** Read the list of words together. Explain that they are all words used on pages 76–77 of the Learner's book. Can the learners find them? Ask the learners to check which letters in the words they have most difficulty writing. They should spend longer tracing these letter shapes and air-writing them. After writing a word once, encourage partners to help each other look for letters they need to improve the next time. They should also think about their pencil grip. Are they using the correct grip? Does it allow them to move the pencil well?

### Success criteria

While completing the activities, assess and record learners who can:

- form letters correctly
- find and spell some familiar words.

### Workbook answers

**Parts of a book**

2. a) caption
   b) contents page
   c) title page
   d) picture

 **IT**

Give the learners access to the Big Wise Owl spelling games on *www.scholastic.co.uk*.

### Further activities

- Learners complete Workbook page 36.
- Give the learners this list of words to find in the text on pages 76–77 of the Learner's book: *make, they, from, with*.

### Assessment ideas

Give the learners, individually, the list of words from *Writing presentation* on page 79 of the Learner's book. Listen as they read them to you. Are they able to copy them with clear letters? Can they spell some of them with only a little help?

# My favourite sport

Pages 80–81

Page 37

## Objectives

- Record answers to questions, e.g. as lists, charts. (1Wa3)
- Speak clearly and choose words carefully to express feelings and ideas when speaking of matters of immediate interest. (1SL1)
- Write for a purpose using some basic features of text type. (1Wa5)
- Read own writing aloud and talk about it. (1WO5)

## Starter

- Direct the learners to the table on page 77 of the Learner's book and remind them how to understand its information.

- Remind the learners that the whole text on pages 76–77 of the Learner's book is a report. Discuss what a report is: it is about a subject; its information does not have to be read in a set order; and it has a varied layout. Draw attention to sentences, headings, labels, pictures, captions and tables.

- Direct the learners to the heading 'Ant colony'. Read the paragraph aloud to the learners, once without pausing at full stops, a second time reading it correctly. Ask: *Which reading was easier to understand?* (The second one.) *What did I do that was different?* Explain that the difference came because you paused at the full stops. Emphasise the importance of writing in sentences and choosing and spelling words carefully.

- Point out the heading at the top of page 80 of the Learner's book: 'My favourite sport'. Talk about sport in your school. Do the learners do other sports outside school? What hobbies do they have outside school? Include such areas as dancing, playing a musical instrument, singing, painting, drawing and reading, and encourage all the learners to contribute to the discussion. As the learners provide information about themselves, use the board as a picture dictionary: write the name of the sport or hobby and do a quick, simple sketch to show what it means. Leave this word bank on the board.

## Activity notes and answers

1. **Gather information.** Direct the learners to the table on page 80 of the Learner's book. Discuss what it shows. Provide the learners with a similar table, the same three headings written, but with three empty rows. Put the learners into groups of four. Explain that everyone must fill in information about the other three learners in their group. Alternatively, the learners could move around the classroom asking three friends of their choice.

**Talk Partners**

**Discuss a favourite sport or hobby.** Direct the learners to the *Talk Partners* box on page 80 of the Learner's book. Read the task before the partners begin. Point out that partners must first tell each other their favourite sport or hobby. Then they take turns asking for the details listed. Remind the learners how to form a question, e.g. *Where do you do your sport?* Emphasise the need for clear questions and answers, and interested listening. Move around the room, helping the learners to form questions.

2. **Write a report.** Read the activity with the learners. Talk about how they will set it out on the page. (They may decide.) Encourage them to make their report look interesting and be informative. What details will be in their picture? What will they draw and label? Suggest a sentence and write it on the board:

*I like … because …*

Let the learners say their sentence aloud, to themselves, a partner or you. Be ready to support spelling with a bank of key words on the board and individual help where needed.

# Getting it right

1. **Get feedback and make changes.** Put the learners into pairs with their completed reports. Deal with one report at a time, reading it aloud. Allow plenty of time for partner discussion and move around offering support before reading the next report.

**What have I learnt?** Advise the learners to read through their report and check to see if they have missed any of these points.

---

### Success criteria

While completing the activities, assess and record learners who can:

- record answers to questions in a table
- talk with a partner about favourite sports or hobbies
- write a simple labelled report
- talk about each other's work and how to improve it.

---

### Further activities

- Learners complete Workbook page 37.
- Ask the learners to create a new table showing the favourite sports or hobbies of three different children.
- Put the learners into groups. Invite them each to read and show their report (activity 2, Learner's book page 80) to the group. What did the others most enjoy about it?

---

### Assessment ideas

Write the checklist from the *What have I learnt?* box on Learner's book page 81. Add a new point: *I have set my report out well.* Ask the learners to colour in a star for each point that they have done.

# Fish to frog

Pages 82–83

Page 38

## Objectives

- Show awareness that texts for different purposes look different, e.g. use of photographs, diagrams. (1Rv1)
- Blend to read, and segment to spell, words with final and initial adjacent consonants, e.g. *b-l*, *n-d*. (1R05)

## Starter

- Choose one learner to stand in front of the class holding the grapheme 'f' and another to hold 'r'. Place both learners facing the class, but standing clearly apart. Ask the class to say their sounds from left to right. Move the learners, and their cards, close together. Ask the class to say their sounds again, this time one immediately after the other so that one grapheme's sound runs smoothly into the next. Explain that this called blending.

- Repeat the last exercise with the graphemes 'b', 'r', 'i' and 'ng'. Invite different learners to hold cards and demonstrate blending by moving the cards together to make 'bring'. Do this again, changing the graphemes to 's', 't', 'i' and 'ng' and blending to make 'sting'. Repeat the exercise with new graphemes so the learners can blend 'crash' and 'flash'.

- Hold up a children's dictionary and show the learner some pages. Ask: *Do you recognise the book? What is it for?* (It lets you check the meaning and spelling of words.)

- Tell the learners that you want to check the word 'tadpole'. Suggest that the dictionary has so many words that it could be difficult to find the one you want. Ask: *How do I know where to go to in the dictionary?* Explain that words are arranged in the same order as the alphabet. (Point to your classroom alphabet.) Ask: *What sound starts this word?* (t) *What letter makes that sound?* ('t') *Where is that letter in the alphabet?* (Near the end.) Demonstrate opening the dictionary near the end and finding 'tadpole'. Show and read the entry. Ask: *How does the dictionary help me?* (It tells you what a tadpole is and how to spell the word.)

- Ask: *Is a dictionary fiction or non-fiction?* (Non-fiction because it supplies facts.) Remind the learners that they have been reading reports recently. Ask: *What do reports look like?* Share ideas, mentioning sentences, diagrams, headings, pictures and photographs, caption and labels and tables.

- Look together at page 82 of the Learner's book. Explain that is a page from a dictionary. Ask partners to tell each other how it looks different from reports. Share ideas as a class, picking out: a list of words all beginning with the same letter; words made to stand out; meanings of the words given; no sentences (so capital letters and full stops are not used). Read the dictionary page aloud as the learners follow. Point out its title: 'Fish to frog'. Ask: *Why is this heading used?* ('fish' is the first word on the dictionary page; 'frog' is the last.)

## Activity notes and answers

**Look at and discuss a dictionary page.** Direct the learners to the *Talk Partners* box on page 82 of the Learner's book. Put the learners into pairs to talk about the page. Direct them to pages 72–73 and 76–77 of the Learner's book to see examples of reports. Give them a storybook. Encourage simple recording of their answers so that you can share ideas later.

# Dictionaries

**Helpful hints:** Point out the *Helpful hints* box on page 83 of the Learner's book. Read it aloud as the learners follow. Ask: *Why does the first word in the dictionary begin with **a**?* (The alphabet begins with *a*.) *Where do words beginning with **z** go?* (The end.) *Where are words beginning with **l**?* (The middle.)

1. **Use a dictionary.** Read the dictionary page on page 82 of the Learner's book as the learners follow. Explain activity 1 on page 83 and suggest that partners work together to find the answers.

   **Answers:**
   a) flame
   b) frog
   c) an animal with smooth skin and webbed feet that lives near water
   d) fork
   e) the pretty part of a plant

2. **Read blends.** Remind the learners what a blend is. Write these blends 'fl', 'fr', 'st', 'sk' and 'tr' on the board. Model saying them for the learners to repeat. Listen and correct as partners say them to each other. Point out that blends may be at the beginning of words, e.g. <u>*sh*</u>*op*; or the end, e.g. *di*<u>*sh*</u>. Let partners work together so that they say the words to each other.

   **Answers:**
   a) flame, flippers, flower
   b) frog
   c) st: still, stick, lost, sty, most
      tr: trick, trim, trill, tree
      sk: ask, tusk, skim, skill

## Further activities

- Learners complete Workbook page 38.

- Make a new bubble of words for the learners to sort into the 'st', 'tr' and 'sk' blends. Put these words in the bubble: flask, trip, step, trot, skin, post, treat, skip, nest.

- Set the learners these questions to answer by using the dictionary text on page 82 of the Learner's book:
  a) Which word is 'a wild animal with red fur and a bushy tail'? (fox)
  b) Which word comes between flower and fork? (football)

- Encourage pairs of learners to read illustrated dictionaries together (see Book list below).

**Workbook answers**

**Dictionary**

1. ant – b, bat – b, chicken – b, drum – b
2. a) chicken, egg, farm
   b) grass, house, igloo
   c) kite, lamb, net

**Success criteria**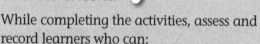

While completing the activities, assess and record learners who can:

- recognise that a dictionary page looks different to a report or a story
- read blends.

**Assessment ideas**

Give the learners a list of words to sort into alphabetical order. You could call the page 'From ant to yak': give these words in a random order to sort: ant, bear, duck, fox, horse, mouse, yak.

**Book list**

- *First Illustrated Dictionary: Key Stage 1, Age 5+* (Schofield and Sims Ltd)

# Alphabetical order

Pages 84–85

Page 39

Learner's book

Workbook

## Objectives

- Know the name and most common sound associated with every letter in the English alphabet. (1R02)
- Answer questions and explain further when asked. (1SL4)

## Starter

- Have a lower case alphabet on display. Show the learners a dictionary. Ask: *What non-fiction book is this? How are a dictionary's words organised?* (In the order of the alphabet.)
- Introduce a game of asking and answering questions. Hold up a bag containing a hidden object. Give individual learners a chance to feel the object (unseen) and ask a question about what it is. Give clear answers. Can someone guess the object?

## Activity notes and answers

1. **Use alphabetical order.** Point out the alphabet on display. Learners may work in pairs.
   **Answers:** a) ask, brick, cup      b) did, egg, fish      c) gull, jug, map

2. **Line up in alphabetical order.** Ask the learners to make a name card for their first name. Put the learners into groups of five to line up in alphabetical order. (Learners may not all be able to do this activity at the same time; some may do it twice.)

**Try this:** Challenge partners to put all nine words in alphabetical order. Give them cards on which to write the words. They can order and then write the answer.

**Answer:** ask, brick, cup, did, egg, fish, gull, jug, map

# Dictionaries

1. **Use a dictionary.** Give each learner a dictionary. (If this is a problem, let half the class do this activity while the others do activity 2.) Explain the instruction and put the learners into pairs.

   **Example answers:**
   foot – part of the body that you walk on.
   bird – an animal that can fly.
   leg – part of the body that holds you up.

2. **Put pictures in alphabetical order.** Put the learners into pairs with drawing materials. Explain that their pictures can be as detailed or simple as they like.

   **Answers:**
   bag, drum, hat

**What have I learnt?** Suggest partners help each other decide how much they know. They should draw one or two smiley faces for each.

## Success criteria

While completing the activities, assess and record learners who can:

- put words in alphabetical order
- answer questions.

## Further activities

- Give the learners groups of three words from the second half of the alphabet to arrange into alphabetical order.
- Learners complete the Self-assessment table on page 39 of the Workbook.

# Playing with rhymes

## Objectives Overview

| Learning Objective | Objective Code | Learner's book Activities | Teacher's pack Activities | Workbook Activities |
|---|---|---|---|---|
| **Reading** | | | | |
| Identify separate sounds (phonemes) within words, which may be represented by more than one letter, e.g. 'th', 'ch', 'sh'. | 1R03 | 91 | 95, 98 | 40 |
| Blend to read, and segment to spell, words with final and initial adjacent consonants, e.g. b-l, n-d. | 1R05 | 87 | 91 | |
| Demonstrate an understanding that one spoken word corresponds with one written word. | 1R07 | 90, 94 | 91, 98 | |
| Join in with reading familiar, simple stories and poems. | 1R08 | 90, 94 | 91, 98 | |
| Read a range of common words on sight. | 1R10 | 90 | 94 | |
| Learn and recite simple poems. | 1R14 | 88 | 91 | |
| Join in and extend rhymes and refrains, playing with language patterns. | 1R15 | 89, 93 | 91 | 41, 44 |
| Read aloud independently from simple books. | 1R16 | | | 41, 42 |
| Talk about significant aspects of a story's language, e.g. repetitive refrain, rhyme, patterned language. | 1Rw1 | 91 | 94 | 42 |
| **Writing** | | | | |
| Form letters correctly. | 1W02 | 89 | 91 | |
| Use relevant vocabulary. | 1Wa2 | 95 | 98 | 44 |
| Spell familiar common words accurately, drawing on sight vocabulary. | 1Ws2 | 93 | 96 | |
| Use rhyme and relate this to spelling patterns. | 1Ws3 | 87 | 91 | 40 |
| **Speaking and listening** | | | | |
| Speak clearly and choose words carefully to express feelings and ideas when speaking of matters of immediate interest. | 1SL1 | 91 | | |
| Show some awareness of the listener through non-verbal communication. | 1SL3 | 92 | 96 | 43 |
| Listen to others and respond appropriately. | 1SL7 | 92 | 96 | |
| Understand that people speak in different ways for different purposes and meanings. | 1SL10 | | | 42 |

# Ice cream cone

Pages 86–89

Pages 40–41

## Objectives

- Use rhyme and relate this to spelling patterns. (1Ws3)
- Blend to read, and segment to spell, words with final and initial adjacent consonants, e.g. *b-l, n-d*. (1R05)
- Learn and recite simple poems. (1R14)
- Join in and extend rhymes and refrains, playing with language patterns. (1R15)

## Starter

- Explain that blends are when the sounds from two or more letters are said together, for example, 'b' 'l' = 'bl'.

- Say the sound made by the blend 'sw' for the learners to imitate. Ask: *Can you think of a word beginning with this sound made by these two letters?* Let partners share suggestions before you share ideas as a class. Write a few examples on the board, e.g. *swan, swap, sway*. Say them together.

- Demonstrate making the blends 'tr' and 'st', choosing learners to hold grapheme cards and demonstrating the blend sound for the learners to imitate. Can the learners think of a word beginning with the new blend sound and those two letters? Write some words on the board, e.g. *train, trick, trip; still, stop, stand*. Say them together.

- Introduce the word *rhyme*. Ask: *What do words that rhyme do?* (They end in the same sound.) Say some oral rhymes: *top* and *hop*; *hair* and *care*. Point out that rhymes do not always have the same spelling.

- Tell the learners that they are going to read poems in the next unit of the Learner's book. Ask: *How is a poem usually set out on the page?* (Poems are usually arranged in lines, and a number of lines may make up a verse.)

- Direct the learners to page 86 of the Learner's book. Point out the poem's layout on the page before you read the title and poem aloud as the learners follow. Direct the learners to the Helpful hints box on Learner's book page 86. Find *sugar* in the poem and practise its pronunciation.

# Rhyming words

## Activity notes and answers

1. **Find blends.** Remind the learners what blends are. Explain that they can be at the beginning, middle or end of a word. Put the learners into pairs. Read a) aloud, direct the learners to page 86 of the Learner's book and wait while they find and write their answers. Do the same for b) and c).

   **Answers:** a) sweet, treat, sticky     b) cold     c) melting

2. **Find sounds and spellings.** Point out the four words to find in the poem. Ask the learners to write them in the same order as on page 87 of the Learner's book. Read aloud the instructions for the learners to do their underlining.

   **Answers:**
   a) sw<u>ee</u>t, tr<u>ea</u>t; dr<u>ip</u>s, t<u>ip</u>s
   b) dr<u>ip</u>s, t<u>ip</u>s

3. **Match rhymes.** Read the list aloud before partners repeat them to each other. They must listen for the words that end in the same sound.

**Answers:**

pips, drips, trips

went, sent, bent

slump, pump, dump

# Playing with rhymes

1. **Answer questions.** Direct the learners to page 86 of the Learner's book and read the poem aloud. Return to the questions on page 88 and read them aloud, one at a time, pausing after each for partners to decide and answer orally to each other. Share answers as a class.

   **Answers:**

   a) It is melting.

   b) Strawberry

   c) They get sticky.

   d) Strawberry ice cream is their favourite treat.

2. **Answer questions about ice cream.** Read the questions aloud. Pause after each for the learners to tell a partner their thoughts. Progress to pictures and writing. Accept single-word answers.

**Talk Partners**  Read, discuss, memorise and perform a poem. Direct the learners to the *Talk Partners* box on page 88 of the Learner's book. Read and discuss the activity. Ask partners to perform to another pair.

# Chocolate bar

1. **Make up a verse.** Put the learners into pairs. Partners may put the lines into the order they prefer. Share ideas before they write the verse.

2. **Read the two verses aloud.** Ask: *What has the person bought?* (A lemon ice lolly.) *What would it be like?* Let partners decide on the missing words and listen for rhymes.

**Writing presentation:** Encourage careful letter formation and an efficient pencil grip.

## Success criteria ✓

While the learners are completing the activities, make a note of who can:

- identify the spelling patterns in words that rhyme
- read blends
- learn and recite simple poems
- write a new verse for the poem.

## Workbook answers

**Follow the rhymes**

1.

| | | | |
|---|---|---|---|
| lost | | hold | fold |
| old | hole | | |
| | coal | gold | ball | cross |
| cold | | | grill | mould | most |
| | bold | cod | hood | rolled |

2. a)  c r o <u>ss</u>

   b)  t r i p

   c)  f l a g

   d)  s t r i <u>ng</u>

   e)  b r i <u>ng</u>

## Workbook answers

**Lizzie**

1.  Lizzie, Lizzie, spinning (top,)
    Ever dancing, never (stop.)
    Dancing in the morning (dew,)
    Barefoot tap, one two, one (two.)

2.  Bang crash bang crash great big drum
    Oh dear now I've hit my **thumb**
    My sister makes the cymbals crash
    My brother gives the blocks a **bash**
    Bang crash bang crash great big drum
    Stop it now – here comes **Mum**

## Further activities

- Learners complete Workbook pages 40–41.
- Ask the learners to write answers to activity 1, page 88 of the Learner's book.
- Return to *Talk Partners*, page 88 of the Learner's book, and invite each pair to perform the poem to a group.
- Can the learners add more rhyming words to each group in activity 3, page 87 of the Learner's book?

# Happy

Pages 90–91

Page 42

### Objectives

- Read a range of simple words on sight. (1R10)
- Talk about significant aspects of a story's language, e.g. repetitive refrain, rhyme, patterned language. (1Rw1)

## Starter

- Remind the learners of the word 'phoneme'. Explain that a phoneme is a sound and that words are made up of a number of sounds put together.

- Say the word *bed* slowly so that the learners can hear each sound in the word. Use your left hand to tally (count) the separate sounds to your thumb and fingers. (For this word, you need to use your thumb and two fingers.)  Say the sounds again. Ask for the children's help as you encode them into writing these graphemes on the board: 'b' 'e' 'd'.

- Repeat the encoding process (changing sounds into graphemes) with another word: say the word *hatch*; tally the word's three sounds on the thumb and two fingers of your left hand; with the learners' help, write these graphemes on the board: 'h' 'a' 'tch'.

- Explain that a word may have any number of phonemes. Suggest that the learners listen and count the phomemes in some words you say aloud. Use these words, and always say them slowly:

  s p oo n  (4)
  l ou d     (3)
  g oa t     (3)
  f or k    (3)

  After the children have answered orally, confirm that they are correct by tallying the phonemes on to your thumb and fingers.

## Activity notes and answers

1.  **Read the poem.** Direct the learners to page 90 of the Learner's book. Ask: *What type of writing do you think this is? Why?* Agree that it looks like a poem because it is set out in lines. Read the poem aloud as the learners follow. Make sure that your face looks happy and your voice is cheerful to suit the poem's message. Read it again, the learners following the lines with their index finger and joining in where they can. Check their understanding of words. Do they know what a kangaroo is? What is a flip-flop? (Be ready to show pictures or a real flip-flop beach shoe.)

# As happy as a ...

1.  **Talk about words in a poem.** Ask the learners to read the poem on page 90 of the Learner's book aloud with a partner and then the class. Support them with some words as needed. Read the questions aloud together. After each, give partners time to find and write answers before moving on. Encourage greater partner discussion of d) and e). Emphasise that there is no correct answer to these last two; they need personal opinion.

    **Answers:**
    a)  happy, as, in, the, a
    b)  happy (5), as (8), in (3), the (3), a (6)
    c)  rainbow, dolphin, kangaroo, buzzy bee, flip-flop, big bass drum

2. **Read words and count phonemes**. Read the list of words with the class. Talk about the instructions and remind the learners how to count phonemes. Use an example from the Starter. Encourage partners to practise reading the words slowly and clearly before they try to count the phonemes. Suggest they take turns saying the word slowly and counting its phonemes.

**Answers:**

a) s-a-n-d (4)     b) r-ai-n-b-ow (5)     c) d-o-l-ph-i-n (6)     d) b-ee (2)

**Talk Partners**

**Discuss feelings created from words in a poem.** Direct the learners to the *Talk Partners* box on page 91 of the Learner's book. Remind the learners what a flip-flop is. Encourage partners to talk about what they would be like to wear and to share personal experiences. Why would these shoes give a happy feeling? Point out that they have no fiddly laces or hard buckles; they are made to go even in water. Could that be why they are happy shoes?

## Success criteria ✔

While the learners are completing the activities, make a note of who can:

* read many words on sight
* answer the questions about the poem.

## Workbook answers

**My mum's sari**

1. a)  mine
   b)  back
   c)  there

## Further activities

* Learners complete Workbook page 42.

* Put the learners into groups of about four to make 'happiness trees'. Their tree should have a branch for each person with a picture of what makes them happy.

* Give the learners more oral practice in counting phonemes. Use these words: *happy, drum, buzzy, shower.*

* Ask the learners to provide an illustration for the poem.

* Find more poems about being happy or doing things that children like (see Book list below) and share these with learners.

**Book list**

* *A First Poetry Book* by Pie Corbett and Gaby Morgan (Macmillan)

* *Rainbow World: Poems from many cultures* edited by Bashabi Fraser and Debjani Chatterjee (Hodder Wayland)

* *Here's a Little Poem* collected by Jane Yolen and Andrew Fusek Peters (Walker Books)

# What a performance

Pages 92–93

Page 43

### Objectives

● Show some awareness of the listener through non-verbal communication. (1SL3)

● Listen to others and respond appropriately. (1SL7)

● Spell familiar common words accurately, drawing on sight vocabulary. (1Ws2)

## Starter

● Encourage the learners to watch and listen to you as you read aloud a short part of a class story. Ask: *Did I make the words clear and interesting? Did I look at you sometimes?* (Make sure that the answer to both questions is yes.) Explain that these things are important to keep listeners' attention.

● Read another story extract, this time from a story with a different mood, perhaps worrying or sad. Make your voice and facial expressions fit the mood. Do the learners notice? Does it help them to be interested?

● Invite the learners to show their partner some writing they have done. Can the partner read it aloud to them? Talk about what helps the partner to know what the words are. Emphasise how helpful correct spelling is.

● Give the learners a spelling tip. They should say the word slowly, identify each sound, and then write the graphemes for those sounds. Point out that there are many words that they know how to spell from seeing and reading them often, and from knowing the sounds that letters make.

● Read aloud 'Happy' from page 90 of the Learner's book, while the learners listen. Remind them to look at you as they show they are interested.

## Activity notes and answers

**Helpful hints:** Read the hints to the learners. Ask: *Did my face match the 'Happy' poem? How?* Invite the learners to show you the happy face they would have when reading this poem.

1. **Read poetry aloud.** Read and explain the activity. Direct the learners to page 90 of the Learner's book and identify the five items mentioned in e). Put the learners into pairs to work out and practise actions. Call out one item at a time for the learners to show their actions. As partners rehearse reading the poem, together and to each other, move about the room offering encouragement and pronunciation help.

2. **Listen to others reading.** Emphasise the importance of all the three points listed. Invite the learners to read the poem to their partner. You could progress to performing for a group or the whole class.

# Having fun with words

1.  **Write what makes them happy.** Read aloud one item at a time, pausing for the learners to decide and write their answer. Afterwards suggest partners compare answers.

    **Example answers:**
    a)  cricket
    b)  a story
    c)  horse
    d)  poppadom
    e)  bicycle

**Helpful hints:** Read the *Helpful hints* box on Learner's book page 93 together and remind them that saying words slowly lets them hear the separate phonemes (sounds). Demonstrate by saying *h a pp y* slowly. Can the learners hear the sounds? Can they write the graphemes to spell the word?

2.  **Write a poem.** Direct the learners to the poem in activity 2 on page 93 of the Learner's book. Ask them to copy it out, filling the empty spaces with their words. Do they need to add other words to make each line make sense?

**Success criteria**

While the learners are completing the activities, make a note of who can:

*   make different faces when talking
*   look interested when listening
*   spell many familiar words.

**Workbook answers**

**Showing your feelings**

1.

a funny poem     a sad poem     an exciting poem

## Further activities

*   Learners complete Workbook page 43.
*   Ask the learners to learn their 'As happy as …' poem by heart (activity 2, Learner's book page 93). Can they think of actions to add to any of the lines?
*   Hold a performance session in which the learners, in groups, perform their 'As happy as …' poems for one another.

**Assessment ideas**

Use the performances of the 'As happy as …' poems to assess how well the learners speak and listen to one another. Watch for eye contact and interested expressions.

# Sampan

Learner's book — Pages 94–97

Workbook — Pages 44–45

## Objectives

- Demonstrate an understanding that one spoken word corresponds with one written word. (1R07)
- Join in with reading familiar, simple stories and poems. (1R08)
- Use relevant vocabulary. (1Wa2)

## Starter

- Remind the learners that they are reading poems in this unit of the Learner's book. Ask: *What do writers often do with the words in poems?* (They repeat them or make some words rhyme.) Explain that when words rhyme they end with the same sound. Provide examples, e.g. *trick* and *brick*; *coat* and *goat*. Point out that rhymes do not always have the same spelling.

- Discuss why the writer repeats words and uses rhymes. Share ideas. Agree that repetition can emphasise the message or mood of the poem; rhyme makes the poem easier to remember and learn by heart.

- Direct the learners to page 90 of the Learner's book. Read the poem aloud together. Ask: *What important word is repeated?* (Happy) *What effect does that have?* (It emphasises the mood of the person in the poem.)

- Direct the learners to page 86 of the Learner's book. Ask them to listen as you read the poem aloud. What do they notice about the sounds of some of the words? (They rhyme.) Help the learners to find the rhymes. Which pair does not spell its rhyming sound in the same way? (*sweet, treat*) Invite the learners to read the poem aloud. Ask: *Do the rhymes help you read the poem?*

- Remind the learners of important things to remember when reading a poem to other people: looking at the listener, using your voice and face to make the words interesting. Direct the learners to page 94 of the Learner's book.

## Activity notes and answers

1. **Join in reading.** Read the poem on page 94 of the Learner's book aloud twice to the learners. Ask them to follow by moving their index finger along the lines as you read. Make sure their finger is always under the correct word. Talk about the meanings of the words in the glossary and any other words that the learners are unfamiliar with. Read the poem aloud again, the learners now joining in as much as they can.

# Fishing boats

1. **Find words in the poem.** Read the activity to the learners. Remind them what a rhyme is. Point out that rhyming words have the same sound but not always the same spelling. Direct partners to the poem on page 94 of the Learner's book.

   **Answers:**
   a) lap, clap, flap, tap, lanterns quiver
   b) lap, clap, flap, tap
   c) river, quiver
   d) They have the same endings: l<u>ap</u>, cl<u>ap</u>, fl<u>ap</u>, t<u>ap</u>; r<u>iver</u> qu<u>iver</u>

2. **Write a poem.** Encourage the learners to read lines aloud to themselves as they write.  Do their lines make sense? Are their lines going to be in the best order for reading their poem aloud?

   **Example answers:**
   **Fishing boat sounds**
   Fishing line squeak squeak
   Fishing boat creak creak
   Jumping fish tumble tumble
   My tummy rumble rumble.

## Success criteria

While the learners are completing the activities, make a note of who can:

- join in with reading the poem
- use the correct vocabulary.

## Workbook answers

**Glorious rain**

1. brain; fast

2. rain    puddles    wet    boots    coat
   mud    splash    umbrella    raindrops

## Further activities

- Learners complete Workbook page 44.

- Put the learners into groups to read their poems from activity 2 on Learners's book page 95 to one another.

- Suggest the learners add a second verse to their poem from activity 2 on Learners's book page 95 What title will they give their poem?

- Ask the learners to investigate repetition in the poems they have written. Which words have they repeated? Have they used any rhyming words?

## Assessment ideas

- Learners complete the Self-assessment table on page 45 of the Workbook.
- Learners complete Quiz 2 on pages 96–97 of the Learner's book. The answers follow on the next page.

## Quiz 2

### Answers:

1.  a)  Pablo and the princess.
    b)  Once upon a time.
    c)  Pablo marries a princess.
    d)  People stick to the goose.

2.  a)  mend
    b)  milk
    c)  trip
    d)  pump

3.  a)  contents page
    b)  caption
    c)  heading

4.  a)  The ball went wide and missed the goal.
    b)  I bought an ice cream and a comic.
    c)  The girl has a red hat and a green coat.
    d)  Sit on the carpet and listen to me.
    e)  The elephant and the zebra drink at the waterhole.

5.  slip – trip
    lent – bent
    hold – bold
    stop – top
    blot – hot
    up – cup

# Fantasy stories

## Objectives Overview

| Learning Objective | Objective Code | Learner's book Activities | Teacher's pack Activities | Workbook Activities |
|---|---|---|---|---|
| **Reading** | | | | |
| Use phonic knowledge to read decodable words and to attempt to sound out some elements of unfamiliar words. | 1R06 | 106, 107 | 110 | |
| Read a range of common words on sight. | 1R10 | 106, 107 | 110 | |
| Enjoy reading and listening to a range of books, drawing on background information and vocabulary provided. | 1R11 | 98 | 102 | |
| Retell stories, with some appropriate use of story language. | 1R13 | 110 | 112 | |
| Read aloud independently from simple books. | 1R16 | 99 | 102 | |
| Pause at full stops when reading. | 1R17 | 100, 101 | 104 | |
| Anticipate what happens next in a story. | 1Ri1 | 101, 108 | 104, 105 | 46 |
| Talk about events in a story and make simple inferences about characters and events to show understanding. | 1Ri2 | 102 | 104 | 47 |
| Recognise story elements, e.g. beginning, middle and end. | 1Rw2 | 109 | 110 | 50 |
| **Writing** | | | | |
| Use knowledge of sounds to write simple regular words, and to attempt other words including when writing simple sentences dictated by the teacher from memory. | 1W04 | 106, 108, 109 | 110 | |
| Read own writing aloud and talk about it. | 1W05 | 115 | 115 | |
| Develop strategies to build vocabulary. | 1W06 | | 110 | |
| Write simple storybooks with sentences to caption pictures. | 1Wa1 | 105, 114 | 108, 109 | |
| Begin to use some formulaic language, e.g. *Once upon a time*. | 1Wa4 | 115 | 115 | 52 |
| Write a sequence of sentences retelling a familiar story or recounting an experience. | 1Wt1 | 111 | 112 | |
| Compose and write a simple sentence with a capital letter and a full stop. | 1Wp2 | | | 47, 49, 52 |
| Write sentence-like structures which may be joined by *and*. | 1Wp3 | 114 | 115 | |
| Begin to learn common spellings of long vowel phonemes, e.g. 'ee', 'ai', 'oo'. | 1Ws1 | 103, 111 | 106, 112 | 48, 51 |
| **Speaking and listening** | | | | |
| Speak clearly and choose words carefully to express feelings and ideas when speaking of matters of immediate interest. | 1SL1 | 98 | 102 | |
| Converse audibly with friends, teachers and other adults. | 1SL2 | 105 | | |
| Take turns in speaking. | 1SL6 | 112 | 114 | |
| Engage in imaginative play, enacting simple characters or situations. | 1SL9 | 102, 104, 113 | 105, 108, 114 | 49 |

# Looking at covers

Learner's book
Pages 98–99

Workbook
Page 46

## Objectives

- Speak clearly and choose words carefully to express feelings and ideas when speaking of matters of immediate interest. (1SL1)
- Enjoy reading and listening to a range of books, drawing on background information and vocabulary provided. (1R11)
- Read aloud independently from simple books. (1R16)

## Starter

- Make sure that you have a large collection of storybooks with covers for the learners to choose from.
- Tell the learners that in this unit of the Learner's book they are going to be reading and writing fiction. Can they remember what fiction is? (A story that is made up.) Ask the learners what sort of stories they like to read. Let partners exchange views before you share opinions as a class.
- Agree that the learners may not have time to look all the way through a book before they decide which book to read in the classroom or to borrow from a library. Ask: *How do you choose a book?* Agree that the book's cover helps.
- Show the learners a suitable cover from a storybook in your classroom. (Choose a clear, informative one.) Ask: *Is this cover helpful? What information does it give you?* Encourage partner talk before you share ideas as a class. Point out the story's title; the name of the writer; the name of the person who has drawn the pictures. Talk about the picture on the cover. What does it suggest that the story is about? Let partners share ideas before you accept answers. Encourage the learners to offer reasons for their opinion.
- Turn to the back cover of the book. Show the learners the text. Ask: *What do you think this writing is about?* (What happens in the story.) Explain that this piece of writing is called the blurb.
- Write 'blurb' on the board. Have the learners seen this word before? Suggest that it is not a word they could just read because they often see it. Ask if they would be able to work it out. How? Remind them of tips for reading new words. They should say the sounds from left to right of the word, and blend the sounds to hear the whole word. Describe how to blend: they point under each grapheme (letter or letter group) as they say the sound; then they run their finger under the whole word as they say the whole (or blended) word.

  e.g. **bl  ur  b      blurb**

## Activity notes and answers

**Helpful hints:** Read the list on Learner's book page 98 to the learners and make sure they understand the labels. Apply the words to the cover shown. Can the learners apply the labels to the appropriate parts of the example cover you have been using?

**Talk Partners**

**Look at and discuss a variety of books.** Direct the learners to the *Talk Partners* box on page 98 of the Learner's book. Give partners access to a number of books with suitably detailed covers. Make sure that there is a blurb on each, and offer adult support with reading it. Encourage partners to express clear views to each other about which book they prefer. Be ready to prompt partner discussion.

# Reading stories

1. **Read aloud.** Suggest that the learners choose about three lines to read aloud. Remind them to obey the pause indicated by a full stop. Sounding out words (blending) will help them read words they do not know. Move among the learners, giving support where needed.

2. **Match titles and characters.** Look together at the three covers and point out the titles. Explain that the characters shown are from these three books. The learners must write the name of each book and the character from it.

   **Answers:**
   a) 'Zee-bot' – f) the alien
   b) 'Anansi Stories' – d) Anansi
   c) 'Dan's Dragon' – e) the boy

**Success criteria**

While completing the activities, assess and record learners who can:

- talk clearly about their thoughts
- talk about the books they like
- read aloud from simple storybooks on their own.

**Workbook answers**

**Story match**

1. a) Bob lands on a red planet. He meets an alien.
   b) Amina finds a baby dragon. They have fun playing together.
   c) Alex fell down a hole and found living dinosaurs.
   d) Three elves live in Tom's garden. They are fun but naughty.

## Further activities

- Learners complete Workbook page 46.
- Let the learners read another part of their chosen book (from the starter activity) to a partner. Can the partner help with problem words?
- Ask the learners to create a new cover picture for the book they have chosen (from the starter activity).
- Read the learners the story of *All Change!,* shown on Learner's book page 98 (see Book list below).

### Assessment ideas

Invite each learner to read a short piece of their chosen book (from the starter activity) aloud to you. Assess their ability to read independently. Can they read some words by sight? Can they sound out other words? Can they tell you how the cover helped them choose this book?

### Book list

- *All Change!* by Ian Whybrow (Hodder Children's Books)

# The Tiger Who Came to Tea

Pages 100–102

Page 47

## Objectives

- Pause at full stops when reading. (1R17)
- Anticipate what happens next in a story. (1Ri1)
- Talk about events in a story and make simple inferences about characters and events to show understanding. (1Ri2)

## Starter

- Tell the learners that writing is divided into sentences. Explain that a sentence is a group of words that makes sense and has a meaning. Agree that they start with a capital letter and end with a full stop.

- Direct the learners to page 52 of the Learner's book and point out the story text. Ask the learners to count the number of sentences in the first paragraph of the story on page 52. How quickly can they tell a partner? Share answers and agree on three. Ask: *Is there an easy way to count the sentences quickly?* Point out the full stop at the end of each sentence. Explain that this is what you counted. Ask: *What else does a sentence need?* (A capital letter at the beginning.)

- Choose a story from the classroom, preferably one unfamiliar to the learners. Read aloud the opening page or two. Put the learners into pairs to tell each other who has been in the story (the characters) and what has happened (the events). Share information and make the learners familiar with the terms 'character' and 'event'.

- Say that there is no time to read any more of the story. Can partners suggest to each other what is likely to happen next? Share ideas as a class. Read aloud a little more of your story. Was anyone right?

- Direct the learners to page 100 of the Learner's book. Point out the story text and its title. Ask the learners to check quickly the number of sentences (Six). Ask: *Does every sentence end with a full stop?* Comment that *Do you think I could have tea with you?* finishes with a different mark. Do the learners recognise the question mark? Point out that a question mark also has a full stop in it. (Point out the 'dot' at the bottom of the question mark.)

## Activity notes and answers

1. **Read aloud.** Ask the learners to listen and follow as you read the story text on page 100 of the Learner's book aloud. Read the text again and this time suggest they use a finger under the words to guide them. On a third reading, ask the learners to join in with you. Do the same with the text on page 101 of the Learner's book to complete the story.

# What happens next?

**Talk Partners** **Discuss what happens next.** Direct the learners to the *Talk Partners* box on page 101 of the Learner's book. Ask the learners to consider what may happen next before they share their ideas with a partner. Encourage them to use the story text on pages 100–101 of the Learner's book for help with spelling characters' names in their sentence.

**Did you know?** Point out the box on page 101 of the Learner's book so that the learners can find out what really happened.

# Talking about a story

1. **Answer questions about a story.** Read the questions aloud to the learners. Remind them what 'characters' means. Encourage the learners to work out and say oral answers to a partner.

   Answers:
   a) Sophie, Mummy, the tiger
   b) A tiger comes when they are having tea.
   c) She says nothing.
   d) He eats sandwiches and buns.

2. **Add to a story.** Be ready to support learners with spellings for their sentence.

**Talk Partners** **Act out a story.** Direct the learners to the *Talk Partners* box on page 102 of the Learner's book. Explain that the learners will act the story as you read it aloud. Pause between sections for the learners to act what has happened. Finally, let group members agree on an ending to act.

## Success criteria ✓

While completing the activities, assess and record learners who can:
* pause at the end of sentences
* suggest what might happen next in the story
* answer questions about the story.

## Book list

* *Mog the Forgetful Cat* by Judith Kerr (HarperCollins Children's Books)

## Further activities

* Learners complete Workbook page 47.
* Invite the groups used in the *Talk Partners* activity on page 102 of the Learner's book to act their story endings for the class.
* Ask some more questions about the story text:
  a) What is the most surprising event in the story?
  b) Is the tiger greedy?
  c) Why doesn't Sophie say anything?
  Ask the learners to give oral answers to a partner before you share ideas as a class. Encourage everyone to speak.
* Read the learners another story by Judith Kerr, the author of *The Tiger Who Came to Tea* (see Book list above).

# Long ai and long ee

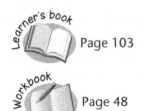

Learner's book **Page 103**

Workbook **Page 48**

## Objectives

- Begin to learn common spellings of long vowel phonemes, e.g. 'ee', 'ai', 'oo'. (1Ws1)

## Starter

- Before you do this spread, make sure that the learners have been introduced gradually to the long vowel phonemes of the alphabetic code. The learners should be able to recognise the sounds and know that their written spellings are not always the same. Regular work with a programme such as *Letters and Sounds* (Department for Education and Skills) will provide the learners with a strong foundation in phonics.

- Explain to the learners that the words you say are made up of sounds called phonemes. The letters and letter groups that are the written code for the sounds are called graphemes. Give the learners a simple example by saying the word *nail*. Can the learners hear the three separate phonemes: *n ai l*? Draw attention to the long vowel sound, saying *ai* again for the learners to repeat. Demonstrate tallying the word's phonemes on the thumb and fingers of your left hand. Ask: *Can you write the graphemes to spell this word?* Let partners help each other before you write the word on the board. Can the learners identify which written letters (graphemes) make the sound *ai*?

- Remind the learners that the **ai** phoneme is not spelt the same in every word. Say *day* to the learners. Can they hear the sound *ai*? Confirm that it is the same long vowel phoneme as the one heard in *nail*. Ask: *Can you write the graphemes to spell this new word?* Let partners help each other before you write the word on the board. Can the learners identify which written letters (graphemes) make the sound *ai*? ('ay') Go through the same exercise with the *ai* sound in the word *cake*. When you write 'cake' on the board, identify 'a_e' as the spelling of the long **ai** phoneme.

- Tell the learners that the long vowel **ee** phoneme also varies its spelling. Say *funny* to the learners. Can they hear the sound *ee*? Ask: *Can you write the graphemes to spell this word?* Let partners help each other before you write the word 'funny' on the board. Can the learners identify which written letters (graphemes) make the sound *ee*? ('y') Separately, say the words *eel, eat* and *even*. Can the learners hear the same long *ee* phoneme? Show them in the written words three other spellings of the sound: 'ee', 'ea', 'e_e'.

## Activity notes and answers

1. **Recognise long vowel phonemes.** Read the activity aloud and explain what has to be done. Point out that the answers are words in the story on pages 100–101 of the Learner's book. Encourage the learners to read and search the story together. Alternatively, you may need to read the story aloud again, partners listening and watching for the words they need. If necessary, direct the learners to a specific paragraph.

   **Answers:**
   a) came, plate
   b) tea
   c) mummy, furry

2. **Sort words with long vowel phonemes.** Read the activity aloud. Read the list of words together, making sure that the learners pronounce them correctly. Suggest that partners work together, saying the words aloud as they decide.

**Answers:**

a) *ai* phoneme

tray, train, crate, tape, pail, lane, stay, rain

b) *ee* phoneme

neat, dotty, eel, tatty, feet, sea, cream, jolly, peep, these

---

**Success criteria**

While completing the activities, assess and record learners who can:

• spell some long vowel phonemes.

**IT**

Visit *www.bbc.co.uk/schools/ wordsandpictures/longvow/index.shtml.* The programme is aimed at Stage 1 learners. There are a number of activities focusing on long vowel sounds.

---

**Workbook answers**

**Playing in the stream**

1. **green – *ai* phoneme**            **red – *ee* phoneme**

   plate                                         stream
   play                                          happy
   say                                           bee
   pale                                          heat
   train                                         deep
   grain                                         flea
   cake                                          coffee
   hay                                           funny

2. Put the words in the table:

| ai spelt ay | ai spelt ai | ai spelt a_e | ee spelt ee | ee spelt ea | ee spelt y |
|---|---|---|---|---|---|
| play | grain | plate | coffee | flea | happy |
| hay | train | pale | deep | heat | funny |
| say | | cake | bee | stream | |

---

## Further activities

• Learners complete Workbook page 48.

• Direct the learners to pages 52–53 of the Learner's book. Ask them to find these words in the story:

   a) two words with the *ai* phoneme spelt 'a_e' (brave, came)
   b) one word with the *ai* phoneme spelt 'ai' (tail)
   c) one word with the *ee* phoneme spelt 'ee' (sleeping)
   d) one word with the *ee* phoneme spelt 'y' (sleepy)
   e) two words with the *ee* phoneme spelt 'ea' (eat, teaching).

# Who is coming to tea?

Pages 104–105

Page 49

## Objectives

- Engage in imaginative play, enacting simple characters or situations. (1SL9)
- Write simple storybooks with sentences to caption pictures. (1Wa1)

## Starter

- Remind the learners that a story has characters in it. Ask: *Who is a character?* (A person or sometimes an animal.) Explain that the story needs characters for its events: characters do things or things happen to them. The characters also make the reader more interested in the story. Suggest that the reader needs to understand the characters. Point out that what characters do and say are the writer's way of telling the reader about a character.

- Direct the learners to pages 100–101 of the Learner's book and read the story aloud as the learners follow. Let the class read aloud the tiger's words. Ask: *What sort of character does the tiger seem to be from his words?* (Polite) *What do his later actions make him seem?* (Rather rude and maybe a bit frightening.)

- Do the same with the two people on pages 100–101 of the Learner's book. Do the learners think that mummy seems surprised that a tiger has come to tea? (No, because she says *Of course.*) What tells the reader that Sophie may be shocked? (She does not say anything.)

- Ask the learners to take the part of Sophie. She decides to speak to the tiger. What does she say? Let partners tell each other what they, as Sophie, would say. Invite some learners to say their words to the class. Extend the role play by asking the learners to take the role of the tiger. Let them show their partner what they would do next. Invite some learners to perform for the class.

- Direct the learners to page 104 of the Learner's book.

## Activity notes and answers

**Talk Partners**

**Act out a story.** Direct the learners to the *Talk Partners* box on page 104 of the Learner's book. Put the learners into pairs and explain that they are going to act. They will choose one scene in which they open a door to a third character. (Point out that on pages 100–101, Sophie and mummy open the door to the tiger.) Read aloud and talk about the options. Share ideas with the learners as they talk to each other in answer to your questions:

a) What would they say to the dragon? Does the dragon damage their house when it comes in?

b) Does the alien understand what they say? Do they make it feel welcome inside their house? Do they both talk?

c) Why do they think the princess has come? Do they try to be friends with the princess? Do they give her some food?

d) Who is the footballer? What do they ask him? Does he play with them?

# Writing a simple story

**Discuss the role play.** Remind the learners of their role play in the *Talk Partner* work on page 104 of the Learner's book. Partners may need to remind each other of what they did before telling the role play stories.

1. **Write a story.** Read the activity to the learners. Emphasise that their pictures should follow the order of what they did in their role play. Be ready to support spelling. A bank of relevant vocabulary on the board will be useful. For other words, remind the learners about saying words slowly to themselves and breaking them into sounds.

**What have I learnt?** Draw attention to the checklist on Learner's book page 105. Suggest that the learners check their stories, point by point. Working with a partner will be helpful.

---

**Success criteria**

While completing the activities, assess and record learners who can:

- take part in role play
- write a simple storybook.

---

## Further activities

- Learners complete Workbook page 49.
- Ask partners to do their acting from page 104 of the Learner's book for the class. Do the learners grow more confident in their role?
- Invite the learners to present their written stories to the class. Ask the audience to think of two questions to ask the reader.

### Assessment ideas

Use a computer to type out the *What have I learnt?* checklist on page 105 of the Learner's book. Add these points to the checklist:

- My pictures and sentences work together to tell the story.
- My character looks interesting.

Print individual copies of this new checklist. Ask the learners to check their story again and give themselves between one and three stars for each point. Talk to the learners about their self-assessment. How would they improve their next story?

# The Way Back Home

Pages 106–109

Page 50

## Objectives

- Read a range of common words on sight. (1R10)
- Use knowledge of sounds to write simple regular words, and to attempt other words including when writing simple sentences dictated by the teacher from memory. (1W04)
- Recognise story elements, e.g. beginning, middle and ending. (1Rw2)
- Use phonic knowledge to read decodable words and to attempt to sound out some elements of unfamiliar words. (1R06)
- Develop strategies to build vocabulary. (1W06)

## Starter

- Remind the learners that a story has three parts. What are they? (Beginning, middle, ending.) Do the learners remember which part is usually the longest? (The middle, because that is when most events happen.) Let them look at their story for activity 1 on page 105 of the Learner's book. Can they think of something else that could happen in the middle part? What details would they add to their middle picture? Invite partners to exchange ideas.

- Talk to the learners about reading stories by themselves. Suggest that there are many words that they know now just by seeing them often. Write some familiar words on the board, e.g. *see, made, dad, mum, house*. Can the learners read them to a partner? Do the partners agree? Read the words aloud together as a class.

- Ask: *How can you try to read and write a word you do not know?* Remind the learners of tips for blending or decoding a word. They should say the sounds from left to right of the word, and blend the sounds to hear the whole word. Describe how to blend: they finger-track under each grapheme (letter or letter group) as they say the sound; then they run their finger under the whole word as they say the whole (or blended) word.

  e.g.  p-ur-p-le  purple

- Read the extract on pages 106-107 of the Learner's book. Write these words from the extract on the board:

  cupboard   aeroplane   petrol   moon

  Play a game where a learner describes a word on the board. He/she is not allowed to use the actual word but should use descriptive language instead. The other learners should guess which word is being described.

  E.g. *This is usually a square or rectangle shape and made of metal or wood. It usually has wooden or metal shelves for putting things on. It has a door on the front.* (Answer: cupboard)

- Write the word *spluttered* on the board and discuss its meaning in the context of the extract on page 107 of the Learner's book. Re-read the extract and ask learners to brainstorm other words that have a similar meaning to *spluttered*, e.g. *gurgled, stopped, shuddered*. Try these new words in the extract instead of *spluttered*.

## Activity notes and answers

1. **Read and spell simple words.** Direct the learners to pages 106–107 of the Learner's book. Ask them to follow as you read the story aloud again. On a second reading, let them follow the lines by having a finger under the word you are reading. On a third reading, invite the learners to read with you. Point out *spluttered* and *petrol*. Do the learners know what they mean? Read aloud the Glossary. Suggest that 'spluttered' is a difficult word to read. Write the word on the board and demonstrate saying the sounds from left to right: *s-p-l-u-tt-er-ed*. Point under each grapheme as you say its sound; then run your finger under the whole word as you say the blended word. Do this again, the learners joining in. Make sure that they hear and say the 'quieter', unstressed *er* sound. Can partners do the decoding together, using the Learner's book? Suggest that the words listed are words they may already know how to read and write. Listen as the class reads the words aloud, correcting where necessary. Partner support will help the learners in this activity.

# A good beginning

1. **Answer questions about a story.** Read the questions aloud. Let partners work together.

   Answers:
   a) The boy finds his aeroplane.
   b) Up in the sky, to the moon.
   c) No, not in an ordinary plane.

2. **Write words.** Remind the learners of tips for encoding or spelling a word. They should say the word slowly to identify each sound in the word. Then they tally each sound to the thumb and fingers of their left hand. Finally, they write down the graphemes for the sounds tallied. Working with a partner will help.

   **Possible answers:** a) queen    b) train    c) sweet    d) sea    e) gate    f) grape

> **Talk Partners**
>
> **Discuss the story.** Direct the learners to the *Talk Partners* box on page 108 of the Learner's book. Read the questions aloud before partners read them again to each other. Encourage both partners to express opinions.

# On the moon

**Helpful hints:** Emphasise that a story often has more than one setting.

1. **Find the setting in a story.**

   Answers:
   a) The boy's house.
   b) cupboard, plane, toys

2. **Answer questions about the story.**
   Answers:
   a) The sky and the moon.
   b) plane, stars, the moon

3. **Think about settings.** Remind the learners that a caption is a sentence or group of words that tell the reader more about the picture.

   Possible captions:
   a) Strange aliens lived on the planet.
   b) The ants had tidy houses under the soil.

> **Workbook answers**
>
> **Lots of settings**
> Palace – princess
> Spaceship – scientist
> Wood – wood fairy
> Underwater kingdom – mermaid

## Further activities

- Learners complete Workbook page 50.
- Direct the learners to the story on pages 100–101 of the Learner's book. Ask them to identify the story's setting.
- Give the learners these words to practise reading quickly and spelling them: *go, have, she, him, this, like.*
- Read the learners the whole story of *The Way Back Home* (see Book list below).

> **Book list**
> - *The Way Back Home* by Oliver Jeffers (HarperCollins Children's Books)

## Success criteria ✔

While completing the activities, assess and record learners who can:
- read some words on sight
- sound out words to write and spell them
- talk about the beginning, middle and ending of a story
- find and use words with similar meanings.

# Retelling a story

Pages 110–111

Page 51

## Objectives

- Retell stories, with some appropriate use of story language. (1R13)
- Begin to learn common spellings of long vowel phonemes, e.g. 'ee', 'ai', 'oo'. (1Ws1)
- Write a sequence of sentences retelling a familiar story or recounting an experience. (1Wt1)

## Starter

- Make the long sound *oo* (as in 'moon'). Describe it as a long vowel phoneme. Explain that *oo*, as with other long vowel phonemes, may vary its spelling. Say the word *moon*. Can the learners hear the three separate phonemes: *m oo n*? Draw attention to the long vowel sound, saying *oo* again for the learners to repeat. Demonstrate tallying the word's phonemes on the thumb and fingers of your left hand. Ask: *Can you write the graphemes to spell this word?* Let partners help each other before you write the word on the board. Can the learners identify which written letters (graphemes) make the sound *oo*? ('oo')

- Go through the same exercise as before with the *oo* sound in the word *chew*. Let the learners tally the phonemes *ch oo*. When you write 'chew' on the board, identify 'ew' as the spelling of the long *oo* phoneme. Say *mule* for the learners. Let the learners tally the phonemes *m oo l*. When you write 'mule' on the board, identify 'u_e' as the spelling of the long *oo* phoneme.

- Provide the learners with tips for encoding or spelling a word. They should say the word slowly so that they can hear each sound in the word. Then they tally each sound on the thumb and fingers of their left hand. Finally, they write down the graphemes for the sounds tallied.

- Remind the learners that this unit is about stories: reading, writing and telling them. Ask: *How should you behave when telling a story?* Talk about the need to talk clearly; to make your voice, facial expression and gestures suit what you are saying; and to make eye contact with the listener. Ask: *How should the listener behave?* Emphasise eye contact with the speaker, paying attention, and being interested.

- Direct the learners to pages 106–107 of the Learner's book. Read the story aloud as the learners follow. Discuss how the story finishes on page 107. Ask: *Is this really the ending of the story?* Suggest that this is still only part of the middle of the story. What do the learners think will happen next?

## Activity notes and answers

**Did you know:** Read the *Did you know?* box on Learner's book page 110 together before the learners complete the *Talk Partners* activity on the same page. Can the learners explain what is happening in each picture?

**Talk Partners**

**Tell a story.** Direct the learners to the *Talk Partners* box on page 110 of the Learner's book. Explain that the pictures show the story on pages 106–107 of the Learner's book, but they also add to it. Remind the learners to speak clearly as they take turns telling the story to each other.

# Writing sentences

1. **Write story sentences.** Remind the learners of their storytelling from the pictures on page 110 of the Learner's book. Draw attention to the fact that some phonemes need two letters when they are spelt.

   **Possible answers:**
   a) The boy was pleased to find his plane.
   b) He flew up to the moon and used up all his petrol.
   c) An alien crashed on to the moon.
   d) The alien gave the boy petrol to fly home.
   e) The boy went back and rescued the alien.

**Helpful hints:** Model the pronunciation of the phoneme and words for the learners to repeat.

2. **Spell words using the long *oo* phoneme.** Let partners work together. Consider giving the learners access to a simple picture dictionary or a bank of words so that they can check their answers.

   **Answers:**

   a) flute     b) screw     c) spoon     d) tube     e) tooth

**Success criteria**

While completing the activities, assess and record learners who can:

- write sentences to retell the story
- complete the words with the correct long vowel phoneme.

## Further activities

- Learners complete Workbook page 51.

- Put the learners into pairs to practise saying, writing and spelling the list of words from activity 2 on page 111 of the Learner's book.

- Direct the learners to the pictures on 110 of the Learner's book. Suggest that one more picture is needed to complete the story. Ask the learners to draw this picture.

- Ask the learners to write a sentence for the picture they have just done. Their sentence must bring the story to an end.

**Assessment ideas**

Individually, ask the learners to do activity 2 on page 111 of the Learner's book again. Check their recognition of the long *oo* phoneme and their understanding that it is spelt with two graphemes (letters).

# Ayo's surprise

Pages 112–113

Learner's book

## Objectives

- Take turns in speaking. (1SL6)
- Engage in imaginative play, enacting simple characters or situations. (1SL9)

## Starter

- Remind the learners that, when speaking to others, you need to talk clearly, use facial expression and gesture to emphasise points, use suitable language and make eye contact with the listener. Ask: *How should the listener behave?* Emphasise eye contact with the speaker, paying attention and looking interested.

- Use the words 'role play'. Do the learners know what the words mean? Define the phrase as taking the part of a character in a story. Emphasise the need to behave and speak as the character in the story would, making up what you say as you go along. Point out the need to react to what other characters do and say.

- Direct the learners to page 112 of the Learner's book. Read the story aloud as the learners follow. Read it a second time, the learners finger-tracking the words as they move along the line you are reading.

## Activity notes and answers

1. **Read a story.** Suggest that the learners first read the story with you, before they read the story together and then to each other.

**Talk Partners**

**Read and discuss a story.** Direct the learners to the *Talk Partners* box on page 112 of the Learner's book. Remind the learners that this is only the beginning of the story, and it has stopped at the end of a page. What Ayo *saw* will be on the next page. Ask the learners to close their eyes and listen as you read the story again. Can they imagine what Ayo saw? Let partners exchange ideas.

# Through the gap

1. **Act out a role.** Read the story aloud from page 112 of the Learner's book. Point out the reference to Ayo going behind the shed. Make sure the learners understand that the place she finds seems different. Read aloud activity 1 on page 113 of the Learner's book and comment on the pictures. Put the learners into pairs. Allow discussion time before the partners act. Move among partners, offering support.

## Further activities

- Divide the class in half, so that some partners act while others watch. Do the learners in the audience recognise the settings?

- Pause the acting so the partners freeze in their situation. Invite some partners to explain who and where they are and to continue their conversation.

## Success criteria ✓

While completing the activities, assess and record learners who can:

- take turns when speaking and listening
- take part in the story role play.

# What happened next?

Pages 114–115

Pages 52–53

## Objectives

- Write sentence-like structures which may be joined by *and*. (1Wp3)
- Begin to use some formulaic language, e.g. *Once upon a time*. (1Wa4)
- Read own writing aloud and talk about it. (1W05)

## Starter

- Emphasise to the learners that their stories should be written in sentences. Remind them that a sentence is a group of words that makes sense and has a meaning. Ask: *How does a sentence begin?* (With a capital letter.) *What ends a sentence?* (A full stop.)

- Explain that *and* is a useful word in a sentence. Can the learners work out why? (It adds more information. Show the learners two sentences on the board, one without 'and', one with.

  *Sophie had tea.*
  *Sophie and her mummy had tea.*

- Remind the learners that they are reading and writing stories in this unit. Suggest that there are some words and phrases (groups of words) that are particularly useful. These often show the order of the story. Ask: *Which words begin many stories?* Let partners share ideas before sharing words as a class. Is 'Once upon a time' the most popular?

- Suggest that there are some words that they know by writing them often; other words they need to work out. Remind the learners of tips for encoding or spelling a word. They should say the word slowly to identify each sound in the word. Then they tally each sound on the thumb and fingers of their left hand. Finally, they write down the graphemes for the sounds tallied. Model this with the word *b ir d*.

- Direct the learners to page 112 of the Learner's book. Read the story aloud with the learners. Remind the learners that the story has not finished; ways that the story could continue are suggested on page 113 of the Learner's book.

## Activity notes and answers

1. **Use *and* in a sentence.** Do this activity one part at a time. Refer the learners to picture a). Then read aloud the half sentence in a) on page 114 of the Learner's book. Wait while the learners decide and say aloud to themselves the rest of their sentence. Give them time to write the whole sentence before progressing to b). Complete the whole activity in this way, supporting spelling as needed.

   **Possible answers:**
   a) Ayo saw the dinosaur and smiled.
   b) Ayo saw the man with the bag and some money.
   c) Ayo landed her spaceship and looked around.
   d) There was a girl in front of a castle and she was waving to Ayo.

2. **Draw pictures to tell a story.** Listen and correct as the learners read the activity aloud. Point out that the middle of the story needs two pictures. Why? (It is where most things happen.)

3. **Writing story sentences.** Treat this writing as an initial draft. Let learners build their own oral sentences. Encourage them to try to write them, but be ready to offer adult support.

# Once upon a time

1. **Find story language.** Put the learners into pairs to find the words. Afterwards, invite learners to tell the class where they are.

2. **Add story language.** Remind the learners about their draft story sentences for activity 3 on page 114 of the Learner's book. They should choose one word or phrase for each section and add them in appropriate places in their sentences. Reading aloud will help them to decide where. Ask them to write their final versions of their sentences.

3. **Share a story.** Encourage thoughtful and helpful comments about each other's work.

**What have I learnt?** Point this list out to the learners when they are doing activity 3 on Learner's book page 115.

### Success criteria

While completing the activities, assess and record learners who can:

- use the word *and* in sentences
- use story language in their story
- read and talk about their own story writing.

### Workbook answers

**Alice in Wonderland**

*Once upon a time* there was a girl called Alice. *One day* Alice was sitting by the river when she saw a white rabbit. "I'm late!" said the White Rabbit. The rabbit went down a hole and Alice followed him. *Suddenly* she was falling. She fell and she fell and she fell. *At last* she reached the ground. The White Rabbit went through a tiny door. "I'm too big!" said Alice. What was she to do?

## Further activities

- Learners complete Workbook page 52.
- Ask the learners to find these words in the story on pages 106–107 of the Learner's book. *Suddenly, Once, Now.* Are they in the beginning or middle of the story?
- Invite the learners to write the story word(s) they would use in the end of the story on pages 106–107 of the Learner's book.

### Assessment ideas

- Use a computer to type out the *What have I learnt?* checklist on page 115 of the Learner's book. Add these points to the checklist:
  - o  drawn pictures that make my story better
  - o  written interesting sentences.

  Print individual copies of the checklist. Ask the learners to check their story again and give themselves between one and three stars for each point. Ask the learners how they would improve their next story?

- Learners complete the Self-assessment table on page 53 of the Workbook.

# Recounts

## Objectives Overview

| Learning Objective | Objective Code | Learner's book Activities | Teacher's pack Activities | Workbook Activities |
|---|---|---|---|---|
| **Reading** | | | | |
| Use phonic knowledge to read decodable words and to attempt to sound out some elements of unfamiliar words. | 1R06 | 130 | | |
| Read a range of common words on sight. | 1R10 | 119 | 120 | 55 |
| Enjoy reading and listening to a range of books, drawing on background information and vocabulary provided. | 1R11 | 118 | 120 | |
| Make links to own experiences. | 1R12 | 117 | 118 | 54 |
| Talk about events in a story and make simple inferences about characters and events to show understanding. | 1Ri2 | 120 | 120 | |
| Show awareness that texts for different purposes look different, e.g. use of photographs, diagrams. | 1Rv1 | 116 | 118 | |
| **Writing** | | | | |
| Read own writing aloud and talk about it. | 1W05 | 123, 131 | 133 | |
| Use relevant vocabulary. | 1Wa2 | 130 | 133 | |
| Write for a purpose using some basic features of text type. | 1Wa5 | 123, 130 | 125, 133 | |
| Write a sequence of sentences retelling a familiar story or recounting an experience. | 1Wt1 | 123, 130 | 125, 126 | 57 |
| Mark some sentence endings with a full stop. | 1Wp1 | 128 | 131 | |
| Compose and write a simple sentence with a capital letter and a full stop. | 1Wp2 | 128, 130 | 131, 132 | |
| Write sentence-like structures which may be joined by *and*. | 1Wp3 | 128 | 131 | 60 |
| Begin to learn common spellings of long vowel phonemes, e.g. 'ee', 'ai', 'oo'. | 1Ws1 | 125, 126, 127 | 127, 129 | 58, 59 |
| Spell familiar common words accurately, drawing on sight vocabulary. | 1Ws2 | 127 | 129 | |
| Recognise common word endings, e.g. *-s, -ed* and *-ing*. | 1Ws4 | 120, 121 | 120, 123 | 56 |
| **Speaking and listening** | | | | |
| Speak clearly and choose words carefully to express feelings and ideas when speaking of matters of immediate interest. | 1SL1 | 124, 129 | 127, 133 | |
| Converse audibly with friends, teachers and other adults. | 1SL2 | 129 | 133 | |
| Speak confidently to a group to share an experience. | 1SL5 | 124 | 128 | |
| Take turns in speaking. | 1SL6 | 129 | 133 | |
| Listen to others and respond appropriately. | 1SL7 | 122, 123 | 125 | |

# Recount

Pages 116–117

Page 54

## Objectives

● Show awareness that texts for different purposes look different, e.g. use of photographs, diagrams. (1Rv1)

● Make links to own experiences. (1R12)

## Starter

● Inform the learners that in this unit of the book they will be reading recount texts. Explain that these are pieces of writing about something that happened to the writer.

● Tell the learners a one-sentence recount of a recent happening in your life, e.g. 'On Tuesday, I needed to stop and put petrol in my car.' Write your recount sentence on the board and read it aloud. Ask: *Who is my recount about? Which word tells you?* (I) Explain that 'I' is often used in a recount. It shows who the story happened to.

● Put the learners into groups of three. Give each group a different musical instrument to play. After a few minutes, collect the instruments. Ask each group to work out a sentence to say together that will tell the class what they did. Ask: *Which two words can you all start with?* Write *We played …* on the board.

● Listen to each group's sentence. Afterwards, confirm that they have all described something that has already happened. Ask: *Why didn't you use 'I'?* (They were talking about three people.) *Which word did you use instead?* (We) Explain that 'I' is just about yourself; 'we' is about yourself and other people.

● Suggest that recounts are often spoken first; they are written down later. Remind the learners of the need to speak clearly, to make eye contact, and to use facial expressions to keep the listener interested. Ask: *What should the listener do?* (Look at the speaker and show interest.)

● Direct the learners to page 116 of the Learner's book.

## Activity notes and answers

**Helpful hints:** Point out this box and read the contents aloud. Emphasise that a recount must be true.

1. **Read recounts.** Point out the pictures on page 116 of the Learner's book. Explain that pictures are often used in a recount text. Read the sentences with the class before partners read them aloud to each other.

# Making links

1. **Tell recounts.** Direct the learners to activity 1 on page 117 of the Learner's book. Read the four recounts as the learners follow the words. Check that the learners understand what happened in each. Suggest that they are all recounts of things that may have happened in the learner's life. Put the learners into pairs. Read recount a) and wait while the learners think of something similar that has happened to them. Ask them to recount it to their partner. Move among the learners, helping and prompting as needed. Invite some learners to tell their recounts to the class. Proceed in the same way for recounts b), c) and d). If necessary, help the learners further by always telling your own similar recount before partners tell each other theirs.

## Success criteria

While completing the activities, assess and record learners who can:

- understand the features of a recount text
- make a connection with their own life.

**IT**

Using activity 1 on page 117 of the Learner's book, make a visual and audio recording of all the learners telling their recounts to others. Afterwards, encourage the class to make constructive comments about how a recount was told and what they most enjoyed.

## Further activities

- Learners complete Workbook page 54.
- Direct the learners to the pictures in activity 1 on page 116 of the Learner's book. Ask partners to tell each other why each picture is used and if it improves the recount.
- Direct the learners to the pictures on page 117 of the Learner's book. Ask partners to tell each other why each picture is used and to comment on how it explains the meaning of the recount.

## Assessment ideas

Listen to the learners telling a recount of something exciting that happened to them on a day out. Listen for their ability to use *I, we, my* and *our* appropriately.

## Stuck in the ice

Pages 118–120

Page 55

Learner's book

Workbook

### Objectives

- Enjoy reading and listening to a range of books, drawing on background information and vocabulary provided. (1R11)
- Read a range of common words on sight. (1R10)
- Talk about events in a story and make simple inferences about characters and events to show understanding. (1Ri2)
- Recognise common word endings, e.g. -s, -ed and -ing. (1Ws4)

### Starter

- Remind the learners that they are reading recounts in this part of the Learner's book. Do they remember what a recount is? Explain that a recount is a true story of something that happened. The recount is told by the person that the things happened to.
- Direct the learners to pages 118–119 of the Learner's book. Read the recount while the learners follow.

### Activity notes and answers

**Talk Partners**

**Read and discuss a recount.** Direct the learners to the *Talk Partners* box on page 118 of the Learner's book. Explain that you will read the recount again. This time, pause between sections for the learners to reread that part aloud with a partner. Let partners share ideas about what particularly interested them.

1. **Read and write words.** Suggest that partners help each other search for the words and practise reading them to each other. Remind them about correct letter formation.

## Word endings

1. **Find answers.** Read the recount on pages 118–119 of the Learner's book aloud while the learners follow and join in where they are able. Explain that the recount contains all the answers to the questions. Put the learners into pairs. Read aloud question a). Read the answer line with the learners, but pause at the empty space for partners to check in the recount text and tell each other the answer. Invite oral answers from some learners and confirm the correct one. Do this for each question. Be ready to guide partners towards the appropriate part of the text, or to remind them that a recount is not made up.

   **Answers:**
   a) The recount is told by Sir Ernest Shackleton.
   b) He wanted to go to the South Pole.
   c) The ship sank.
   d) The island was called Elephant Island.
   e) It is true.

**Helpful hints:** Remind the learners that a root word is a starting word. Explain that a root word can add letters when it needs to: *-ed, -ing,* and *-s* are often added. Point out the new, longer words in the box on Learner's book page 120 that have been made this way. For each, read the new word aloud. Ask half the class to read its root word aloud; the other half of the class must read and say the added ending.

## Success criteria

While completing the activities, assess and record learners who can:

- say what makes the recount interesting
- read some words on sight
- answer questions about the recount.

## Workbook answers

### Common word search

1.

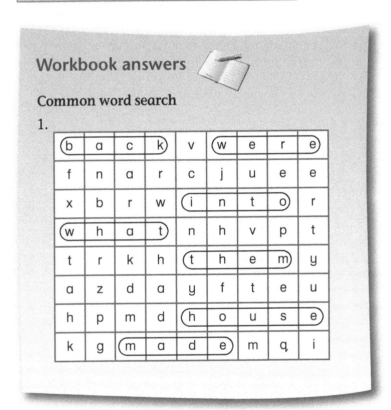

IT Look at *www.bbc.co.uk/historic_figures/shackleton_ernest.shtml* for further information about Shackleton's voyage to the South Pole.

## Further activities

- Learners complete Workbook page 55.
- Ask the learners to find these words in the recount and to practise reading them to a partner and writing them: *sank, small, pulled, was.*
- Supply new questions for the learners to answer by reading the recount:

  a) Where did the ship become stuck?

  The ship became stuck _____ (in the ice.)

  b) What was Elephant island like?

  Elephant Island was _____ (small and empty.)

  c) How did the men make a house on Elephant Island?

  They made it from _____ (a boat.)

# Adding *-ed, -ing* and *-s*

Page 121

Page 56

**Objectives**

- Recognise common word endings, e.g. *-s, -ed* and *-ing*. (1Ws4)

## Starter

- Remind the learners that a root word is a starting word. It often adds an ending to make a new word.

- Explain that different endings may be added to a root word. Copy the endings *-ed, -ing* and *-s* on to three separate, large cards for three learners to hold. On a different card, write the root word 'land'. Invite another learner to stand holding the card and face the class. Can the class read the word? Give a + sign to a learner and ask them to stand next in line. Invite the learner with the *-ed* ending to stand next to the + sign. Ask: *What is the new, longer word?* Help the class to read 'landed'. In turn, do this with the other endings, the class reading the words. Repeat the game with a new root word, 'walk', and different learners holding the cards.

- Say and write the word 'played' on the board. You and another adult demonstrate separating the root word from its ending, one of you writing 'play' on a piece of card, the other person writing *-ed*. Stand side-by-side but slightly apart, holding your word and ending and facing the class.

- Write these sentences on the board: *We were playing games and singing songs lots of the time. We pulled our gloves over our fingers and pushed our hats over our eyes.* Read the text aloud. Explain that there are some words here with *-ed, -ing* and *-s* endings. Put the learners into pairs to find one word for each ending. Give them sufficient time before you share findings as a class. Underline the answers: playing, games, singing, songs, lots, pulled, gloves, fingers, pushed, hats, eyes. Allocate a different underlined word to each pair of learners. (Some pairs of learners may need to have the same word.) Writing on individual whiteboards or pieces of paper, the learners must separate the root word from its ending. Invite each pair of learners to present their results to the class.

- Direct the learners to pages 118–119 of the Learner's book. Read the recount aloud, drawing attention to the words ending in *-ed* in the final section on page 119. (Under the heading 'Elephant Island'.)

## Activity notes and answers

1. **Separate root words and endings**. Ask the learners to read the list of long words a) to g) aloud. Direct the learners to pages 118–119 of the Learner's book. Read the recount aloud, drawing attention to the listed words when you reach them. Put the learners into pairs to reread the recount, find the words and separate the root word from its ending. Show how the answers must be written in the completed example in activity 1.

   **Answers:**

   a) pulled = pull + ed

   b) played = play + ed

   c) climbed = climb + ed

   d) sailed = sail + ed

   e) eating = eat + ing

   f) weeks = week + s

   g) songs = song + s

2. **Add endings.** Encourage the learners to choose the most appropriate ending. Looking at the pictures and counting letter spaces will help.

   **Answers:**

   a) eggs   b) jumping   c) kicked   d) sings

### Workbook answers

**–ed, –ing, –s**

1. a) Yesterday, we went rid(ing) in the park.

   b) She look(ed) out of the window for her friend.

   c) My father sing(s) in the morning.

   d) Josh play(s) with his brother.

   e) The bird is fly(ing) up high.

   f) I have plant(ed) a cherry tree.

2. a) Yesterday, we went swimm**ing**.

   b) Last week we went on a picnic but it rain**ed**.

   c) We jump**ed** over the stream.

   d) The girl runs to school.

   e) I am cook**ing** lentils for lunch.

### Further activities

- Learners complete Workbook page 56.
- Let the learners find these words on pages 118–119 of the Learner's book: stayed, seals, reached, games. Can the learners separate the root word and ending? (stay + ed; seal + s; reach + ed; game + s)
- Ask the learners to build new words: play + ing; boat + s; climb + ing; jump + ed (playing, boats, climbing, jumped).

### Success criteria

While completing the activities, assess and record learners who can:

- recognise some common word endings and add endings to words.

### Assessment ideas

Provide each learner with a list of words and incomplete addition sentences. Read the words aloud to the learners. Give them pencils of two colours. Ask them to split the words into the root word and ending by underlining the two parts correctly. (Agree which colour is for the root word and which colour for the ending.) Afterwards ask them to complete the addition sentences by writing each root word and its ending.

opened

.............. + ..............

cakes

.............. + ..............

eating

.............. + ..............

buns

.............. + ..............

rained

.............. + ..............

standing

.............. + ..............

chairs

.............. + ..............

drinking

.............. + ..............

# My day out

Pages 122–123

Page 57

## Objectives

- Listen to others and respond appropriately. (1SL7)
- Write for a purpose using some basic features of text type. (1Wa5)
- Write a sequence of sentences retelling a familiar story or recounting an experience. (1Wt1)

## Starter

- Remind the learners that this part of the Learner's book is about recounts. Ask: *What is a recount?* (A true story about something that happened to the writer or speaker.) Explain that a recount may be spoken or written.

- Suggest that recounts are often spoken first; they are written down later. Ask the learners how they should tell a recount. Share ideas, talking about the need for clear, audible speech, eye contact with the listener, and appropriate facial expressions to keep the listener interested. Ask: *What should the listener do?* (Look at the speaker, show interest, and be ready to comment or ask questions afterwards.)

- Talk about another lesson in a different subject earlier that day or the day before. Choose a lesson where many activities were taking place. Recount what you did in the lesson, for example, 'I sat with the green group and we counted with cubes'. Put the learners into pairs to tell each other what they did in that lesson. Afterwards ask the partners to tell each other if and how well they heard them. Did the speaker think the listener was paying attention? Encourage partners and the class to share ideas for improving their speaking and listening.

- Direct the learners to page 122 of the Learner's book. Point out the subheading 'My day out'. Ask them to think of a day out they had with their family. Wait while everyone remembers one. Be ready to use a special school day if any learners cannot think of one.

- Put the learners into pairs.

## Activity notes and answers

**Discuss a day out or event.** Read and explain the speaking frame on Learner's book page 122 to the learners. Ask partners to take turns telling each other about their day out, using the sentence starters in that order.

**Ask questions.** Point out the instructions to the listener. Suggest asking one or two questions.

**Recount the story.** Partners must try to remember details as they tell the recounts back. Afterwards, discuss how well the listeners did.

# Writing my recount

1. **Write a recount.** Read instruction a) aloud, point out the picture, and demonstrate folding your piece of paper for the learners to copy. Let the learners read the sentence starters aloud before copying them, one in each section, in the order given. Can they remember how they finished the sentences when they told their recount? They must finish the sentences now in writing. The learners may find it helpful to sit with their partner from their oral recount: they can remind each other of what they said.

2. **Read and check recounts.** Remind the learners that a capital letter must begin every sentence, and a full stop end one. Encourage them to share spelling knowledge and their recognition of sounds.

**Try this:** Remind the learners to use the sentence starters on Learner's book page 123 in the correct order. Suggest saying an oral sentence aloud, to themselves or to a partner, before they write it.

**Success criteria**

While completing the activities, assess and record learners who can:

- listen to a partner and ask relevant questions
- recount an event.

**Workbook answers**

**The pony ride**
a) One day, I went on a pony ride.
b) The pony stopped to eat apples.
c) Dad made a line of apples.

**IT** Let the learners watch and listen to recounts by famous people of famous events in history. Visit *www.scholastic.co.uk* and search for 'I was there'.

## Further activities

- Learners complete Workbook page 57.
- Invite the learners to share their written recount (activity 1, Learner's book page 123) with a new partner. Suggest partners listen to each other and ask a question about the recount.
- Put the learners into reading groups to each read aloud their recount. Encourage the listeners to each say what they liked about it.
- Ask the learners to learn to spell these words: first, next, then, saw, one, day. Suggest using the LSCWC (look, say, cover, write, check) method to learn.

**Assessment ideas**

Ask each learner to read their recount (activity 1, Learner's book page 123) to you. Consider:

- Do the sentence endings make sense?
- Has the learner understood the task?
- Have I/we/my/our been used correctly?
- Do the pictures match the recount text?

# The school trip

Pages 124–125

Page 58

## Objectives

- Speak clearly and choose words carefully to express feelings and ideas when speaking of matters of immediate interest. (1SL1)
- Begin to learn common spellings of long vowel phonemes, e.g. 'ee', 'ai', 'oo'. (1Ws1)

## Starter

- Explain to the learners that the words you say are made up of sounds. Remind them that these sounds are called phonemes. The letters and letter groups that are the written code for the sounds are called graphemes. Give the learners a simple example by saying the word 'make'. Can the learners hear the three separate phonemes: *m ai k*? Draw attention to the long vowel sound, saying *ai* again for the learners to repeat. Demonstrate tallying the word's phonemes on the thumb and fingers of your left hand. Ask: *Can you write the graphemes to spell this word?* Let partners help each other before you write the word on the board. Can the learners identify which written letters (graphemes) make the sound *ai*? ('a_e')

- Tell the learners that the *ai* phoneme is not spelt the same in every word. Say 'day' to the learners. Can they hear the sound *ai*? Confirm that it is the same long vowel phoneme as the one used in 'make'. Ask: *Can you write the graphemes to spell this new word?* Let partners help each other before you write the word on the board. Can the learners identify which written letters (graphemes) make the sound *ai*? ('ay')

- Remind the learners that they have been reading and telling recounts. Ask: *What is important when you speak to someone?* (Making yourself heard and talking clearly.)

- Direct the learners to page 124 of the Learner's book. Read the recount aloud as the learners follow. Draw attention to these words: lake, coach, bliss. Can the learners tell a partner their meanings? Agree that a lake is a large body of water; a coach is a bus; and bliss means perfect happiness.

- Reread the account, the children following each line with their index finger under the words.

## Activity notes and answers

1. **Retell a recount.** Read the recount on pages 124–125 of the Learner's book aloud as the learners read with you. Pause frequently to comment on or question the learners about important points. Ask: *How did the school children travel? Was it hot or cold on the coach? Where did the children go? What did they do with the water? Were they happy?* Read the activity instructions aloud for partners to do. Suggest that afterwards they tell each other if they could hear and understand them.

2. **Use long phonemes.** Remind the learners about the long *ai* phoneme (sound). What is difficult about changing this sound into written graphemes? (There are different spellings.) Read the instructions for activity 2 on page 125 of the Learner's book aloud and explain what has to be done. Point out that the answers to a) and b) are words in the recount on pages 124–125 of the Learner's book. Encourage the learners to read and search the recount together. Alternatively, you may need to read the recount aloud again, partners listening and watching for the words they need. Make sure that the learners can read and pronounce correctly the words in c).

   Answers:
   a) lake
   b) way, Friday
   c) spelt 'ay': clay, day, tray, play, stay
      spelt 'a_e': name, plane, fake, pale, cake

### Success criteria ✓

While completing the activities, assess and record learners who can:

- speak clearly
- spell long vowel phonemes.

**IT** Go to *www.scholastic.co.uk* and search for 'Slips and Slimes'. Print out a copy of the sheet. The learners will be able to look for examples of different long vowel phonemes and write them in the ready-made table.

### Workbook answers

**Long vowel phonemes**

1.  a) snail
    b) paint
    c) hay
    d) snake
    e) wave

2.  a) leaf
    b) heel
    c) ear
    d) wheel
    e) bee

### Further activities

- Learners complete Workbook page 58.

- Ask the learners to make two new columns for the long *ai* vowel phoneme, using the same headings as in activity 1 c) on page 125 of the Learner's book. Give them these words to read with a partner and write in the correct columns: game, may, bake, ray, plate, say, tale, pay, take, lay.

- Put the learners into pairs to reread the second part of the recount on page 125 of the Learner's book. Can they each tell their partner what happened? Are they talking clearly? Can their partner hear them?

# Cool, fool and tool

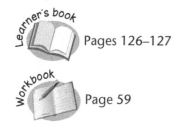

Learner's book
Pages 126–127

Workbook
Page 59

## Objectives

● Begin to learn common spellings of long vowel phonemes, e.g. 'ee', 'ai', 'oo'.  (1Ws1)

● Spell familiar common words accurately, drawing on sight vocabulary. (1Ws2)

## Starter

● Remind the learners that the spoken sounds in words are called phonemes. Give the learners a simple example by saying the word 'coat'. Can the learners hear the three separate phonemes: c *oa* t? Draw attention to the long vowel sound, saying *oa* again for the learners to repeat. Demonstrate tallying the word's phonemes on the thumb and fingers of your left hand. Ask: *Can you write the graphemes to spell this word?* Let partners help each other before you write the word on the board. Can the learners identify which written letters (grapheme) make the sound *oa*? (*oa*).

● Tell the learners that the *oa* phoneme is not spelt the same in every word. Say 'home' to the learners. Can they hear the sound *oa*? Confirm that it is the same long vowel phoneme as the one used in 'coat'. Ask: *Can you write the graphemes to spell this new word?* Let partners help each other before you write the word on the board. Can the learners identify the split digraph which makes the sound *oa*? ('o_e' is split by the letter 'm').

● Introduce the *oo* phoneme by saying 'pool'. Ask: *What is the long vowel sound?* (*oo*). Can the learners write the word? Can they identify the grapheme that makes the *oo* phoneme? (*oo*). Warn the learners that the *oo* phoneme is not spelt like this in every word. Say 'tune'. Can the learners hear the *oo* sound? Do they know how to spell the word? Write 'tune'. Explain that 'u_e' makes the *oo* sound. This is a split digraph.

● Direct the learners to pages 124–125 of the Learner's book. Read the recount aloud as the learners follow and join in sometimes. Pause sometimes to comment on or question the learners about important happenings in the recount. For example, ask: *Why did the water sparkle? Did the children have any lunch? What did they do on the way home?*

## Activity notes and answers

1. **Show understanding of a recount.** Make sure that the learners understand that 'true' means correct; 'false' means wrong. Suggest that the learners read each statement in turn, check in that part of the recount on pages 124–125 of the Learner's book to find what happened, and then write 'true' or 'false'. Partner work will be helpful.

   **Answers:**  a) false      b) false      c) true      d) false      e) true

**Helpful hints:** Read the contents of the box on Learner's book page 126 aloud. Ask the learners to say the phonemes. Can they say the example words correctly? Point out the grapheme 'ow' to represent the *oa* phoneme, and the grapheme 'u_e' for the *oo* phoneme. Ask: *How many different ways have we now found to spell each phoneme?* (Three)

2. **Find words with long vowel phonemes.** Explain the activity. For question a) direct the partners to page 124 of the Learner's book; for questions b) and c) direct them to page 125. Some learners may need guiding to a particular sentence or paragraph.

   **Answers:**  a) coach      b) home      c) food

# Spelling words

1. **Recognise long vowel phonemes.** Read the phonemes for the learners to repeat. Read the bubble of words together, making sure they are all pronounced correctly. Help the learners to prepare a table of two columns. Explain that the first two words are written for them to copy. Put the learners into pairs, so that they can remind each other how to pronounce the words.

   **Answers:**

   **oa** words: boat, coach, float, flown, grow, home, stove, hope, flow, coat.

   **oo** words: cool, school, pool, tool, balloon, huge, tune, flute, newt, grew, stew, hoop.

2. **Spell words with long vowel phonemes.** Ask the learners what each picture represents. Agree on the words for each one. Put the learners into pairs to say the words to each other. Can they hear phonemes they know? Do they remember how to spell them? Are there some words they can spell easily?

   **Answers:**

   a)  spoon

   c)  over

   e)  blow

   b)  snow

   d)  moon

   f)  bone

### Success criteria

While completing the activities, assess and record learners who can:

* spell long vowel phonemes
* spell the words correctly.

### Workbook answers

**Three in a row**

a)  goat, snow, hope

b)  blew, fool, cute

c)  say, game, stay, plane, train

d)  feet, neat, steam

## Further activities

* Learners complete Workbook page 59.

* Ask the learners to learn to spell these words by using the LSCWC (Look, say, cover, write, check) method: food, room, school, move, new. Can the learners hear what sound all the words have? (The **oo** phoneme.)

* Direct the learners to pages 118–119 of the Learner's book. Ask them to find:

   a)  a word with the long **oa** phoneme spelt 'o_e'. (pole)

   b)  a word with the long **oa** phoneme spelt 'oa'. (boat)

   c)  a word with the long **oo** phoneme spelt 'ew'. (new)

* Let the learners answer 'true' or 'false' to these statements. They will need to check the recount on 124–125 of the Learner's book.

   a)  The children put their feet in the lake. (false)

   b)  The children went on a train. (false)

   c)  Some swans wanted lunch too. (false)

   d)  The children slept on the way home. (true)

# Practising sentences

Pages 128

Page 60

**Objectives**

- Mark some sentence endings with a full stop. (1Wp1)
- Compose and write a simple sentence with a capital letter and a full stop. (1Wp2)
- Write sentence-like structures which may be joined by *and*. (1Wp3)

## Starter

- Tell the learners that writing is divided into sentences. Remind them that a sentence is a group of words that makes sense and has a meaning. Write, separately, these two groups of words on the board:

    a)  to a lake

    b)  we went to a lake

    Ask: *Which group of words can be a sentence?* (b) Leave b) on the board.

- Direct the learners to page 124 of the Learner's book and point out the recount text. Ask the learners to count the number of sentences in the recount on page 124. How quickly can they tell a partner? Share answers and agree on three. Ask: *Is there an easy way to count the sentences quickly?* Point out the full stop at the end of each sentence. Explain that this is what you counted. Ask: *What else does a sentence need?* (A capital letter at the beginning.)

- Return to your group b) words on the board. Can the learners tell you what to do to make the words into a proper sentence? (Begin 'We' with a capital letter; add a full stop after 'lake'.)

- Write this group of words on the board:

    left school and the lake we went to

    Ask the learners to read your line of words aloud. Does the line make sense? (No) Can the learners put the words into a sensible order to make them into a sentence? Let partners share ideas before you order the words together. Write the answer on the board:

    we left school and went to the lake

    Ask: *What do we still need to do to make the words into a sentence?* Change 'we' so that it begins with a capital letter; put a full stop after 'lake'.

- Ask the learners to say when and why the word *and* is used. Explain that it is used in a sentence to add more information. It tells the reader, or listener, that you are saying more than one thing. Write some example sentences on the board:

    a)  My Mum and I went to the supermarket.

    b)  We bought food and went home.

    c)  We cooked and ate the food.

    Underline *and* in each sentence. Can the learners tell you what extra information is joined on?

## Activity notes and answers

**Helpful hints:** Read the box on Learner's book page 128 aloud. Ask about the use of capital letters. Can the learners tell a partner which words need capital letters? Explain that capital letters are used for the start of a sentence and for other special words. These special words are: days, months, the names of people and places, and 'I' on its own. Ask: *Why does 'I' needs a capital letter?* (It is the name of myself.) Direct the learners to page 118 of the Learner's book and point out the capital letters for the explorer (Sir Ernest Shackleton) and the place (South Pole). Move to page 124 of the Learner's book and point out a day (Friday).

1. **Make sentences.** Explain the first activity on Learner's book page 128. Suggest partners work together as they order the words. Remind them to add a capital letter and a full stop to their sentence.

   **Answers:**
   a) We went to the lake and ate lunch.
   b) My sister took me to the park and we had an ice cream.
   c) I opened the door and went inside.

2. **Write sentences.** Discuss the pictures. Ask: *Is it a boy or girl in picture a)? What could the child's name be? Could it be you? Why do you think the person is having a drink?* Question the learners about picture b). Ask: *Where is the cat? Why is it sleepy? How does the cat feel? Is it making a noise?* Encourage partners to exchange ideas before they write a sentence for each picture. Suggest trying to use *and*.

   **Example answers:**
   a) I was thirsty and I needed a drink.
   b) My cat slept and purred in the sun.

### Success criteria

While completing the activities, assess and record learners who can:

- use a full stop to end a sentence
- use the word *and* to add information.

IT Use 'Jigsaw sentences' from *www.scholastic.co.uk*. The activity asks learners to rearrange jumbled words into sentences.

## Further activities

- Learners complete Workbook page 60.
- Ask the learners to draw three pictures to match the sentences in activity 1 on Learner's book page 128.
- Give the learners two new pictures to write sentences for. The pictures could show:
  a) two ducks eating someone's lunch
  b) a boy asleep under a tree.

### Assessment ideas

Give the learners the following to complete.

**Find the missing word in the box and write it in the correct place.**

| me | and | start | name | end |
| --- | --- | --- | --- | --- |

a) A capital letter goes at the _____ of a sentence.

b) A full stop goes at the _____ of a sentence.

c) A capital letter is used for 'I' because it is a _____ for _____ .

d) You can use _____ to say more than one thing.

# Do you remember?

Pages 129–131

Page 61

## Objectives

- Take turns in speaking. (1SL6)
- Speak clearly and choose words carefully to express feelings and ideas when speaking of matters of immediate interest. (1SL1)
- Write for a purpose using some basic features of text type. (1Wa5)
- Use relevant with language patterns. (1Wa2)
- Read own writing aloud and talk about it. (1WO5)
- Converse audibly with friends, teachers and other adults. (1SL2)

## Starter

- Remind the learners that they have been reading recounts in this unit of the Learner's book. Talk about a recount's features: it is a true account of something that happened; it is usually told by the person in the story, so 'I' and 'we' are likely words.

- Explain that the events in a recount should be told in the order in which they happened. Point out that many useful words and phrases (groups of words) can be used to emphasise the sequence of events. Direct the learners to page 123 of the Learner's book. Point out the first and last sentence beginnings in activity 1 b). Suggest that these provide a useful way to start and finish a recount.

- Talk to the learners about school trips you have made with them, perhaps to a park or museum. Discuss when it took place, what the learners saw and did, something unusual, funny or exciting that happened during the trip, how the day ended. Suggest that they could write a recount of this. Ask them to look at pages 124–125 of the Learner's book again. Ask: *What helps to keep the reader interested?* (A mixture of words and pictures.) Suggest that they do the same in their recount.

## Activity notes and answers

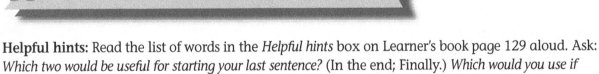

Talk Partners

**Discuss a school trip.** Remind partners to take turns speaking and listening to each other.

**Helpful hints:** Read the list of words in the *Helpful hints* box on Learner's book page 129 aloud. Ask: *Which two would be useful for starting your last sentence?* (In the end; Finally.) *Which would you use if something surprising happened?* (Suddenly.) *Which would you choose to start the recount?* (One day.)

1. **Tell an oral recount.** Read the starters together. Emphasise that the learners are saying not writing the sentences.

# Our trip

1. **Make a recount picture book.** Demonstrate folding a piece of paper into five sections to make a zigzag book. Point out the picture as you help the learners do this. Remind the learners of the five sentences that they told their partner about their trip (activity 1, page 129 of the Learner's book). Ask them to draw five pictures in the same order as those sentences.

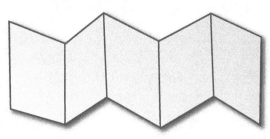

2. **Tell a recount of a trip from pictures.** Remind the learners to use some of the useful words from page 129 of the Learner's book. Emphasise that they should use the proper names for the place they went to and what they saw. Encourage them to practise saying their five sentences more than once.

3. **Write a recount of a trip.** Remind the learners to spell words carefully. Saying words aloud slowly will help them hear the different phonemes.

# Sharing work

1. **Read and check their own recount.** Encourage the learners to read their recount more than once.

2. **Share their recount.** Emphasise the need to read and speak clearly, and to make helpful comments.

**What have I learnt:** Read the list on Learner's book page 131 aloud to the learners. Remind them where capital letters and full stops should be used. Suggest that they read each point and then look for that mistake in their recount.

### Further activities

- Ask the learners to share their recount (activities 1–3 on Learner's book page 130) with a new partner. Do the learners learn new things about their writing? What do they most enjoy in their new partner's recount?

- Invite some learners to read and show their recounts to the class. What do the listeners like? Are the recounts very different?

### Success criteria ✓

While completing the activities, assess and record learners who can:

- take turns when speaking
- talk clearly about their thoughts
- write sentences to tell a recount
- use the correct vocabulary
- read and talk about their own writing to improve it.

### Assessment ideas

- Type and print individual copies of the checklist on page 131 of the Learner's book. Ask the learners to assess how pleased they are with their recount book. Suggest that they award themselves between one and three stars for each point on the checklist.

- Learners complete the Self-assessment table on page 61 of the Workbook.

# Unit 9 Animal poems

## Objectives Overview

| Learning Objective | Objective Code | Learner's book Activities | Teacher's pack Activities | Workbook Activities |
|---|---|---|---|---|
| **Reading** | | | | |
| Identify separate sounds (phonemes) within words, which may be represented by more than one letter, e.g. 'th', 'ch', 'sh'. | 1R03 | 132, 139 | 136, 137, 142 | |
| Demonstrate an understanding that one spoken word corresponds with one written word. | 1R07 | 132, 136, 140 | 136, 142 | |
| Join in with reading familiar, simple stories and poems. | 1R08 | 132, 136, 140 | 136, 137 | |
| Learn and recite simple poems. | 1R14 | 134 | 138, 139 | |
| Join in and extend rhymes and refrains, playing with language patterns. | 1R15 | 134, 135 | 138 | 63 |
| Read aloud independently from simple books. | 1R16 | | | 64, 68, 69 |
| Talk about significant aspects of a story's language, e.g. repetitive refrain, rhyme, patterned language. | 1Rw1 | 139 | 140 | 64, 65 |
| **Writing** | | | | |
| Know that a capital letter is used for *I*, for proper nouns and for the start of a sentence. | 1W03 | | | 65 |
| Use knowledge of sounds to write simple regular words, and to attempt other words including when writing simple sentences dictated by the teacher from memory. | 1W04 | 137 | 140 | |
| Use relevant vocabulary. | 1Wa2 | 141 | 143 | |
| Begin to learn common spellings of long vowel phonemes, e.g. 'ee', 'ai', 'oo'. | 1Ws1 | 139 | 142 | 66, 67 |
| Use rhyme and relate this to spelling patterns. | 1Ws3 | 133, 135 | 136, 138 | 62 |
| Recognise common word endings, e.g. *-s, -ed* and *-ing*. | 1Ws4 | 137 | 140 | |
| **Speaking and listening** | | | | |
| Speak clearly and choose words carefully to express feelings and ideas when speaking of matters of immediate interest. | 1SL1 | 138 | | |
| Understand that people speak in different ways for different purposes and meanings. | 1SL10 | 142 | 142 | 68, 69 |

# Chimpanzee

Pages 132–133

Page 62

## Objectives

- Demonstrate an understanding that one spoken word corresponds with one written word. (1R07)
- Join in with reading familiar, simple stories and poems. (1R08)
- Use rhyme and relate this to spelling patterns. (1Ws3)
- Identify separate sounds (phonemes) within words, which may be represented by more than one letter, e.g. 'th', 'ch', 'sh'. (1R03)

## Starter

- Explain to the learners that they will be reading new poems in this part of the Learner's book. Suggest that they will know some words, but they may not recognise others. Ask: *How can you try to read a word you do not know?* Remind the learners of tips for blending or decoding a word. They should break the word into phonemes (sounds) and say the phonemes from left to right of the word, and then blend the phonemes to hear the whole word. Describe how to blend: they finger-track under each grapheme (letter or letter group) as they say the sound; then they run their finger under the whole word as they say the whole (or blended) word.

  e.g. p-ur-p-le   purple

- Remind the learners that a phoneme can vary its spelling. Make the sound *ee* (as in 'seat'). Say the word *seat*. Can the learners hear the three separate phonemes: *s ee t*? Demonstrate tallying the word's phonemes on the thumb and fingers of your left hand. Ask: *Can you write the graphemes to spell this word?* Let partners help each other before you write the word on the board. Can the learners identify which written letters (graphemes) make the sound *ee*? ('ea').

- Go through the same exercise as before with the *ee* sound by saying the word *me*. Let the learners tally the phonemes *m* and *ee*. When you write 'me' on the board, identify 'e' as the spelling of the long *ee* phoneme. Emphasise that there are many other spellings for the *ee* phoneme.

- Use the word 'rhyme'. Do the learners know what it means? Give the learners some examples: *cat* and *mat*; *feel* and *meal*; *me* and *bee*. Define rhyme as words that end with the same sound. Suggest that poems often have rhyming words.

## Activity notes and answers

1. **Read aloud.** Direct the learners to page 132 of the Learner's book and read the poem aloud. Put the learners into pairs. Watch that the learners are pointing to the word they are reading.

2. **Break words into phonemes.** Encourage partners to help each other blend the phonemes to hear the whole word. Move among the pairs, offering support.

**Did you know?** Point out this box on Learner's book page 132. Encourage partner and class discussion. Do the learners know other facts about chimpanzees? (They live in the jungle. They usually walk on all fours; this is called knuckle-walking. In many ways, they are like people. Chimpanzees eat lots of different foods: fruit, nuts, insects and sometimes meat.)

# Rhyming words

1. **Answer questions about a poem.** Read the first question aloud. Wait for the learners to find and tell a partner the answer. Invite oral answers from individuals. Treat the other questions in the same way.

   **Answers:**
   a) They swing.
   b) They eat nuts and fleas.
   c) They munch them off each other.

2. **Recognise rhymes.** Model the *ee* phoneme for the learners to repeat. Read aloud and explain each section. Let the learners work in pairs.

   **Answers:**
   a) chimpanzee, trees, eat, fleas, each, we
   b) trees, fleas
   c) bees, knees, breeze
   d) feet, beat

**Workbook answers**

**Spelling match**

1. a) hike – bike
   b) flight – light
   c) power – flower
   d) grain – chain
   e) frame – flame
   f) roads – toads
   g) glow – arrow

**Success criteria** ✓

While completing the activities, assess and record learners who can:
- read along with the poem
- recognise the spelling patterns in words that rhyme.

## Further activities

- Learners complete Workbook page 62.
- Remind the learners of their oral answers to activity 1 on page 133 of the Learner's book. Ask them to write the answers.
- Ask the learners to sort these words into those that rhyme with *trees* and those that rhyme with *eat*. Underline the parts of the words that rhyme.

  neat, sneeze, meet, fleas, cheese, heat

- Read *Rumble in the Jungle* (see Book list below) to the learners and encourage them to spot the rhyming words.

### Assessment ideas

Question each learner individually. Ask: *What does rhyme mean?* Can they say another word to rhyme with *chimpanzee*? (me) Can they find two rhyming words in the poem on page 132 of the Learner's book?

### Book list

- *Rumble in the Jungle* by Giles Andreae (Orchard Books)

# Jungle animals

 Pages 134–135

 Page 63

## Objectives

- Learn and recite simple poems. (1R14)
- Join in and extend rhymes and refrains, playing with language patterns. (1R15)
- Use rhyme and relate this to spelling patterns. (1Ws3)

## Starter

- Remind the learners that they are reading poems in this unit. Ask: *Are you able to say any poems without reading them?* Remind them about nursery rhymes they are likely to know. Invite them to recite some.

- Ask: *How did you learn the words?* Let partners exchange tips for learning by heart before you share ideas as a class. Talk about: listening to others reading the poem; reading it yourself; reading it many times; spotting words that are easy to remember; practising saying the lines.

- Use the word 'rhyme'. Do the learners remember what it means? Define rhyme as the use of words that end with the same sound. Do the learners think that poems with rhyming words may be easier to learn by heart? Why? Suggest that having just said one sound, we are likely to remember it and be ready to repeat it.

- Explain that sounds that rhyme do not have to be spelt in the same way. Say these words to the learners: happy, me, sea, bee, monkey. Ask: *Do the words rhyme?* (Yes) *How can you tell?* (They all end with the same sound.) Say the words again for the learners to tell you what the rhyming sound is (*ee*). Now write the words on the board for the learners to read aloud. Can partners work out which letters in each word make the *ee* sound. Invite answers and underline graphemes in the words in this way: happ<u>y</u>, m<u>e</u>, s<u>ea</u>, b<u>ee</u>, monk<u>ey</u>. Point out that the *ee* phoneme is spelt differently in each of these words.

- Direct the learners to page 132 of the Learner's book and read the poem aloud again.

## Activity notes and answers

1. **Learn a poem by heart.** Put the learners into pairs, and then go through each part of the activity with them. Encourage partners to listen to and help each other. Repeat the activity more than once until learners feel confident about saying the words.

   **Answers:**

   d) trees, fleas

   e) 2. Swinging through the trees
      4. We munch each other's fleas!

   f) 1. It's great to be a chimpanzee
      3. And if we can't find nuts to eat

# Jungle poem

1. **Pair rhymes.**

   **Answers:**

   sun – run, leaves – trees, pool – cool

2. **Complete the poem.** Suggest that the learners say lines aloud before they write the completed poem. Emphasise that the missing words are all in the bubble.

   **Answers:**

   It's great to be an elephant
   Munching at the leaves
   And if I can't quite reach them
   I just knock down the trees.

   It's great to be a lion
   Sleeping in the sun
   When I wake, I give a roar
   And watch the zebra run.

   It's great to be a hippo
   Bathing in a pool
   Even in the hot, hot sun
   It keeps me very cool.

**Success criteria**

While completing the activities, assess and record learners who can:

- learn and recite a poem
- write the new verses for the Jungle poem.

**IT**

Use the 'Rhyming pairs' sheet from www.scholastic.co.uk. Helped by a picture and word labels, the learners must find the rhyming pairs.

## Further activities

- Learners complete Workbook page 63.

- Put the learners into small groups to recite 'Chimpanzee' to a new partner. Let each group rehearse saying the poem so that they can recite it to the class.

- Direct the learners to page 90 of the Learner's book. Read the poem aloud. Ask the learners to identify the rhymes. Put the learners into pairs and, following the order of work in activity 1 on page 134 of the Learner's book, ask them to learn 'Happy' (or part of it) by heart and recite it to a partner.

### Assessment ideas

Give the learners a bubble of words to pair into rhymes. Ask them to use the words to complete this poem.

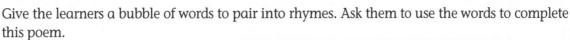

lake        by        ground        sky        shake        round

It's great to be a giraffe
My head up in the _____ (sky)
I spy on all the animals
And wave as birds fly _____ (by).

It's great to be a snake
Sliding up and _____ (round)
When I'm tired of climbing trees
I go back on the _____ (ground).

It's great to be a crocodile
Splashing in the _____ (lake)
And if I see a little frog
I make him shiver and _____ (shake).

## Mice

Learner's book Pages 136–138

Workbook Page 64–65

**Objectives**

● Recognise common word endings, e.g. –s, –ed and –ing. (1Ws4)

● Talk about significant aspects of a story's language, e.g. repetitive refrain, rhyme, patterned language. (1Rw1)

### Starter

● Remind the learners that they are reading poems in this unit. Suggest that not everyone likes the same poems. Ask the learners if they have a favourite nursery rhyme. Share partner and then class views, encouraging the learners to have opinions of their own. Invite learners to explain why they like a particular nursery rhyme. Suggest that it is usually the words used that appeal to the reader.

● Direct the learners to pages 132 and 135 of the Learner's book, and read or recite the poems with them. Write the names of the two poems in two different colours on the board. Give the learners two pieces of card of the two colours of the poem titles. Explain that they are going to tell you which poem they like best by holding up that colour card. Count the cards shown for each poem and write the numbers on the board. Invite learners to pick out favourite words or lines in the poem they chose.

● Mention 'rhyme'. Do the learners remember what it means? Define rhyme as the use of words that end with the same sound. Do the learners like poems with rhyming words? Emphasise that sounds that rhyme do not have to be spelt in the same way. Demonstrate this by writing 'funny' and 'chimpanzee' on the board. Say the words aloud. Ask: *Do the words rhyme?* (Yes) *How can you tell?* (They end with the same sound.) Draw attention to the different spelling by underlining the letters that make the rhyming *ee* sound: 'funn<u>y</u>', 'chimpanz<u>ee</u>'.

● Use the term 'root word', defining it as a starting word. Remind the learners that a root word may add an ending (e.g. –ed, –ing and –s) to make a new word. Explain that in the next poem they are going to read, –s has been added to many root words. Write 'tree' on the board for the learners to read aloud. Ask: *What new word will be made by adding '–s'?* Write 'trees' on the board. Ask: *What has adding '–s' done to the meaning of the word?* (It has made the word mean 'more than one'.) Do this again with the words 'lion' and 'elephant'. Next to the words, draw pictures of single animals. Add –s and write 'lions' and 'elephants'. Next to the new words, draw two lions and three elephants.

● Direct the learners to page 136 of the Learner's book and read the poem aloud as the learners follow.

## Liking mice

### Activity notes and answers

**Helpful hints:** Make sure that the learners notice that 'thing' has become 'things', and 'face' has become 'faces'.

2. **Write words.** Agree on what the pictures represent.

Answers:

a) one ball

b) two balls

c) one hat

d) four hats

e) one bee

f) three bees

# Finding patterns

1. **Find rhymes.**

   **Answers:**
   a) small – all
   b) white – night
   c) touch – much
   d) mice – nice

2. **Find word repetition.** Suggest that words are often repeated in a poem. Do the learners think that they make a poem easier to remember?

   **Answers:**
   a) At the beginning and end of the poem.
   b) They have long tails and small faces. They have pink ears and white teeth.
   c) They run about the house at night. They nibble things they shouldn't touch.

## Success criteria

While completing the activities, assess and record learners who can:

* spot words ending in –*s* in the poem
* find rhyming and repeated words in the poem.

 Amazon Media's Kindle Edition of *Mice* by Rose Fyleman (Beach Lane Books) has an audio recording. This will allow the learners to hear how one line of the poem often runs into the next.

**Talk Partners**  Read and discuss a poem. Read the poem on Learner's book page 136 aloud as the learners follow; then let partners read together. Remind the learners to give each other a chance to speak and to listen to their views about the poem.

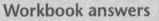 

## Workbook answers

**Questions about Little goat**

1. a) little goat
   b) Candice went
2. a) A girl
3. a) white
   b) Candice
   c) Follows Candice
4. a) Candice went, Candice went
   b) And everywhere that Candice went
   c) The goat was sure to go.
5. The capital letter is for a name.

## Further activities

* Learners complete Workbook pages 64–65.
* Make a worksheet with appropriate drawings and these incomplete labels. Ask the learners to write the missing words:
  a) one … (house)
  b) two … (houses)
  c) one … (cat)
  d) three … (cats)
  e) one … (shoe)
  f) four … (shoes)
* Put the learners into groups of about four to practise reading the poem on Learner's book page 136 aloud together. Invite them to recite it to the rest of the class.

# Long vowels

Pages 139–144

Pages 66–70

**Objectives**

- Begin to learn common spellings of long vowel phonemes, e.g. 'ee', 'ai', 'oo'. (1Ws1)

- Understand that people speak in different ways for different purposes and meanings. (1SL10)

## Starter

- Point out that in this unit the learners have been talking about poems as well as reading and writing them. Direct the learners to page 132 of the Learner's book and read the poem aloud in a clear voice. Ask for comments on the way you are talking. Do even the furthest learners away hear what you are saying?

- Put the learners into pairs to tell each other what they like about the poem. Afterwards, suggest that their talk was quieter than yours because they were talking to a friend next to them. Explain that you change the way you talk to fit: the occasion; who you are talking to; what you are talking about.

- Remind the learners that a phoneme is a sound in speech. Make the long sound *ee* (as in 'heat'). Say the word *heat*. Can the learners hear the three separate phonemes? Demonstrate tallying the word's phonemes on the thumb and fingers of your left hand. Ask: *Can you write the graphemes to spell this word?* Let partners help each other before you write the word on the board. Can the learners identify which written letters (graphemes) make the sound *ee*? ('ea')

- Go through the same exercise as before with the *ee* sound by saying the word *happy*. Let the learners tally the phonemes: *h a p ee*. When you write 'happy' on the board, identify 'y' as the spelling of the long *ee* phoneme. Emphasise that there are other spellings for the *ee* phoneme.

- Make the long vowel *ai* phoneme. Say the word *aim*. Can the learners hear the two separate phonemes: *ai m*? Demonstrate tallying the phonemes on the thumb and finger of your left hand. Ask: *Can you write the graphemes to spell this word?* Let partners help each other before you write the word on the board. Can the learners identify which written letters (graphemes) make the sound *ai*? ('ai')

- Repeat the exercise with the *ai* sound by saying the word *take*. Let the learners tally the phonemes: *t ai k*. When you write 'take' on the board, identify 'a_e' as the spelling of the long *ai* phoneme. Make sure they understand that the *ai* sound is made by two letters, but the digraph is split by the 'k'. Emphasise that there are many other spellings for the *ai* and other long vowel phonemes.

- Direct the learners to page 136 of the Learner's book and read the poem aloud in a clear voice as the learners follow.

## Activity notes and answers

1. **Read long vowels.** Model the phonemes for the learners to repeat.

   **Answers:**

   a) teeth, seems    b) mice, nice    c) night    d) tails    e) faces

2. **Sort long vowels.** Listen to the learners read the words aloud and correct pronunciation.

   **Answers:**

   | igh | ee | ai | oa | oo |
   |------|-----|------|-----|-----|
   | like | see | make | no | too |
   | I | we | day | | |
   | time | | | | |

# Snake in school

1. **Read aloud.** Talk about the word 'monsoon' in the glossary. Ensure all the learners understand what it means and how to say it.

# Different types of talk

1. **Draw and write about a poem.** Read the activity to the learners. Remind them to say words slowly to themselves.

   **Example answer:** The snake was chased out of the school gate.

 **Talk Partners**

Discuss different types of talking. Put the learners into pairs. Read aloud a) and allow one to two minutes for partners to share ideas. Invite some feedback to the class before moving to b). Complete all the work in this way.

**Example answers:**
a) They chat quickly in happy voices.
b) The child uses a clear voice, saying words carefully.
c) You speak quietly in a sad voice.

## Success criteria ✓

While completing the activities, assess and record learners who can:

- identify long vowel phonemes
- explain how people talk in different situations.

2. **Read and perform a poem.** Put the learners into pairs and encourage them to think about how they are talking as they read the poem out loud. They should have loud, clear voices and look like they are enjoying the poem.

## Workbook answers

### Spelling choice

1. a) plain   b) trail   c) stay
   d) green   e) bee

2. a) crow
   b) goat
   c) boat
   d) snow

### The Hippopotamus Song

1. four times

2. hollow, wallow

### Long vowel search

| n | f | v | t | i | l | e | k | h | w |
|---|---|---|---|---|---|---|---|---|---|
| s | l | i | m | e | d | J | u | l | y |
| h | n | m | q | h | f | i | m | m | d |
| l | g | w | f | l | y | b | q | y | f |
| b | i | t | e | s | o | r | w | h | h |
| i | x | z | k | r | h | i | g | h | q |
| t | w | h | i | l | e | g | t | r | y |

## Further activities

- Learners complete Workbook pages 66–69.
- Let partners act situations from the *Talk Partner* box on page 141 of the Learner's book. Each must take a turn as speaker.

## Assessment ideas

- Learners complete the Self-assessment table on page 70 of the Workbook.
- Learners complete Quiz 3 on pages 142–144 of the Learner's book. The answers follow on the next page.

# Quiz 3

## Answers:

1. a) the beginning

   b) Bert and Ernie

   c) a coral reef

2.

| ai | ee | igh | oa | oo |
|---|---|---|---|---|
| pain | seem | flight | float | pool |
| plain | beat | cry | hole | tune |
| plate | | bite | snow | |

3. a) They went to the seaside.

   b) They could not have a picnic or make a sandcastle.

   c) They jumped and splashed in the waves.

   d) recount

4. a) flying

   b) packed

   c) girls

5. **Possible sentences**

   a) Ruby is eating an apple and Kofi is eating a banana.

   b) We go to the funfair and have fun.

6. a) ice cream

   b) skating

   c) screw

   d) night